MW00577261

FORECLOSURES
UNLOCKED

A CHOOSE YOUR OWN ADVENTURE BOOK

FORECLOSURES UNLOCKED

YOUR KEY TO SUCCESS IN REAL ESTATE INVESTING

TWO GUYS TAKE ON REAL ESTATE

FORECLOSURES UNLOCKED
YOUR KEY TO SUCCESS IN REAL ESTATE INVESTING

Written by Matthew "The Flippin' Landlord Ninja" Tortoriello and Kevin "The Property Prince" Shippee

Published and distributed by Merack Publishing
San Diego, USA
www.merackpublishing.com

Library of Congress Control Number: 2023903827
Matthew Tortoriello and Kevin Shippee
Foreclosure Unlocked: Your Key to Success in Real Estate Investing

Paperback: ISBN 978-1-957048-88-8
Casebound: ISBN 978-1-957048-89-5
eBook: ISBN 978-1-957048-90-1

To anyone who wakes up thinking they could
never make money buying a real estate foreclosure.

CONTENTS

INTRODUCTION

If you're reading this, then you've probably considered buying a foreclosure. Maybe you've heard that buying foreclosures is a good way to acquire property on the cheap, but you've wondered where to begin. Like a lot of people, you might have thought about buying a foreclosure but stopped because it seemed wicked risky or too complicated, or even too good to be true. If this sounds familiar, then we wrote this book for you.

Or maybe you think foreclosure-buying is an easy way to make a quick buck and anybody could do it, so you're reading a book or two before diving in with both feet. If this sounds like you, then we wrote the book for you too.

That's because buying property at a foreclosure auction is not for the faint of heart. It can be a huge risk and things can go massively wrong. A lot of people wouldn't buy a property at a foreclosure auction because it can be incredibly sketchy. You never know what you might have to deal with. We've bought some ridiculous stuff, and we've seen everything. We once bought a house at auction only to find out later that it had a homeless couple living in it. Separating from them took six months of coordinating with social services, as well as thousands of dollars in court costs. Another time we bought a multifamily house that turned out to have a u-porn studio in the basement. And don't even get us started on the one with the goat in a bedroom.... So, a lot of people would say, "Yeah, I'd love to buy a house in foreclosure, but it's way too risky. There's no way in hell!"

Then there are the people we've run into at some auctions, money in hand and ready to bid on a house with people living in it. Everyone's standing on the front lawn of a place that's clearly occupied. Nobody's getting to see inside the house. And yet you can hear the noobs talking amongst themselves as they bid. "Well, the people are going to be gone when we buy it, right?"

Nope. No, they're not. In fact, dealing with occupants is often a huge component of buying a property at a foreclosure auction. You don't even know who the people living there are then. Are they the owners? Are they rent-paying tenants who have every legal right to live in the house? Are they crackheads there to steal the plumbing? Again, you don't know what's going on. Is there even a working heating system in that home?

So, there are the people who think, "Hey, I'll just buy a house. It's going to be super easy." Or there are people like, "Wow, I don't know anything about foreclosures. It's so risky. I would never do something like that. I've heard all these horror stories. I would never want to buy a foreclosure." We're gearing this book toward both types. To the person who thinks it's super easy, we say, "Whoa, hit the brakes there, pal. It's not as easy as you think." And to the person who says it's way too hard, we say, "Well, hit the brakes there, pal. It doesn't have to be as hard as you think, either."

We're here to say that buying foreclosures can be a path to acquiring a great property cheaply, so you might want to consider it. We'll show you how we do it. We'll tell you about our adventures and a lot of our mistakes because let's face it, the horror stories are more fun to talk about than the happy endings. But really we hope our stories teach you both how to make money buying discounted property this way and the many ways to lose money if you're not prepared, if you're not creative, or if you can't pivot your game plan when you need to.

The idea of this book is to make buying property at a foreclosure auction accessible. To folks who say, "I don't have time or money to deal with mistakes," you don't have to. You can hit the ground running a little bit easier than we did instead of running through a minefield all on our own, blindfolded. We've made a path through the minefield, and yeah, it's still dangerous. Nobody wants to run through a fricking minefield, but at least you can know where the last guys went and you can kind of follow behind them and have an easier go of it. Why wouldn't we want to help somebody avoid what we went through to find success? We wish we'd had somebody we could've followed. We would've saved ourselves some limbs!

When we started out, we wanted—we needed—a book like this one, but until now it didn't exist. There are other books on foreclosure buying, but none talk about what you should *not* do as well as what you *should* do. So we decided to write one ourselves. The whole idea behind the book actually started back when we started. When we had only a couple of apartments, folks who were then real estate giants took the time to mentor us instead of viewing us as competitors who would take business from them. They considered us colleagues and fellow entrepreneurs and helped us avoid some of the mistakes they made. We're here to pay it forward and to teach you from all the mistakes we've made so you don't have to make those same mistakes.

We're going to explain the whole process of buying a foreclosure, from finding a prospect to performing due diligence, to attending an auction, to dealing with occupants once you close the deal, to ultimately getting the keys to the property free and clear. Along the way we'll talk about the risks and the many—oh, so many—ways a deal can go wrong. We know because we've been there. We're going to share with you the strategies and tactics you can follow just like we have to profit from buying a foreclosure, even if the deal starts going south. We'll explain how we assess a prospective property based on our goals for it. We'll describe how we approach the actual auction to maximize our chance of winning without overpaying. We'll also tell you about the tragedies and trainwrecks that cost us time and money. We'll explain how we overcame more surprises and challenges than we can count. And we'll share the lessons we've learned along the way to building a successful real estate business.

We've now bought, renovated, flipped, rented, and managed over 700 units in western Massachusetts and northern Connecticut. We both live in beautiful houses that we acquired in foreclosure auctions. But when we started out fifteen years ago, we had none of that. We had just graduated from college. Kev was a communications major and Matt was pre-med, so naturally we went into real estate! Kev had never bought property before. Matt had already bought two properties, one that made him a small profit and a second that became, shall we say, a "learning opportunity." But with those two deals, Matt got the real estate bug and then convinced Kev to join him.

It was 2008. The real estate market was crashing, which was ironically a good time to be getting in. We'll talk more later about what makes for a "good foreclosure market" and why now is as good a time as any for a noob, but at that time Matt started looking at a hundred homes a week as possible investments. At first we looked at properties our agent found on the Multiple Listing Service or "MLS," but we just couldn't make the numbers work to a level where we were comfortable with the cash flow. We quickly realized that we needed to focus instead on distressed property that we could buy at a discount to market value.

We also realized that if we went the traditional route and bought a house with a mortgage from a conventional bank that required our original investment be tied up in the property, it would take us a long time to build a sustainable business. Conventional banks would lend us money based only on the current market value of a property at the time we bought it. And once we'd bought it, we'd have to start again saving up money for another down payment, hope and pray there were no (expensive) problems with the first property in the meantime, and wait a year or two before we could afford to buy the next one.

But if we could find a lender that would make us a loan based on after repair value (ARV) rather than current market value, we could keep our money free from being tied up in the property. With our money freed up, we could buy another property quickly. Buying and renovating a distressed property rather than a turnkey property, there would be a good chance that after we finished the rehab we could pull out all of our original investment—at first we didn't realize we'd be able to pull out more than that—go buy another property to rehab, and do the same thing over and over. Maybe we could buy a couple houses a year.

At least, that was our thought. Matt was already working on real estate full-time; he didn't want to buy and reno one house, then go find a job doing something else to make ends meet, and then buy the next house a couple years later. He wanted to keep buying properties. So we knew we had to buy a distressed property where we could add value.

In 2008 there were so many properties being foreclosed in our town of Springfield, Massachusetts, that you couldn't go anywhere without seeing a truck loaded with plywood driving around boarding up houses. It was crazy. Our real estate agent worked with one of the area's top REO agents. An REO, which stands for "real estate owned," is a property that a bank bought back for itself at a foreclosure auction, and the bank usually wants to unload it quickly. Often banks will funnel all their REOs to a small handful of agents in the area who specialize in these properties. A lot of agents, then and now, wouldn't deal with distressed properties for reasons that will become clear from our stories. But Mary Grace had brass balls. She wasn't afraid of anything. She started taking us to properties that could work for our strategy, which was to buy a distressed property at a discount, renovate it, rent it, and then refinance it to pull out our equity so that we could invest in the next property.

Our first purchase together was an REO duplex. We got a hard money loan—which we'll explain a little later—and put down $15k with the intention of fixing the house up ourselves. We had no idea what we were getting into. We would show up at the property and then watch YouTube videos trying to figure out how to do whatever we needed that day: paint this or scrape that, or demo this or install that. Matt worked all day on the house; Kev worked on the house before and after working another day job. He'd wear crappy clothes to the rehab, and then change into a shirt and tie before going to his day job. After work he'd go back to the house and change back into crappy clothes. Most nights we both worked until midnight, mostly because we just didn't know what we were getting ourselves into when it came to rehabbing a house. We were like, "Oh hey, we'll paint it." But we didn't know how to estimate our costs that well at all.

We ended up putting in an incredible amount of time on that property because, well, we were stuck. We owned the house, and it needed repair work. And our tight budget meant that we had to be the ones to do it. We realized pretty quickly that we bit off more than we could chew.

We could see that we were going way over budget because the property needed much more work than we expected. Our solution was to work harder, and that became the way we operated for the next couple of years. When we ran into a problem, we just had to work longer hours, put in more effort, more time, more sweat, and fix our mistakes through maximum effort, as Deadpool would say. That way of working happened over and over and over. Whatever it was that set us back, our response to it was to work eight days a week (cue music). Eventually we did set some limits for ourselves, like stopping work at 7:30 at night, because we realized we had to have a life outside of rehabbing houses. It took us three months of twelve-hour-plus days to get that first house in shape to rent, and we still own it to this day.

Since then, we've made every mistake in this book. But we've also made a good living for ourselves and our families, provided job security for our employees, and built a successful company that provides rental housing for hundreds of families in communities throughout Massachusetts and Connecticut. Now we want to share our experiences with you so that you don't have to go through what we've been through.

One of the biggest lessons we learned is that foreclosure buying is always an adventure. The stuff that happens, you just can't make up. Sue the occupants for eviction? Bam, you just got countersued! Found a vacant foreclosure you're ready to flip? Wham, somebody's living in the barn! Just closed on that Victorian fixer-upper in the country? Surprise, there's a hundred-year-old oil tank buried in the yard! Ready to close on that fix-and-flip you thought would take three months? Whoops—it just burned down! You think we're making all this up. We're not.

The first section explains the rules of the road. We'll explain a little more about the opportunities you can find in the foreclosure market, explain exactly what a foreclosure is and how you find them, and teach you how to think like a foreclosure buyer. The second section is where the real fun begins: You get to try your hand at buying a foreclosure. So that you can experience the same kind of adventure we've been on for years, we've written this section in a "choose your own foreclosure" style. Your objective is not to go broke—or worse. Maybe you'll decide not to bid at all. Maybe you'll walk away from your deposit. Maybe you'll spend a bunch of money and time evicting a recalcitrant former owner who refuses to leave. Or maybe, you'll play your hand right, follow our advice, and end up with a vacant property that's ready for the next step in your strategy. The last section is some parting wisdom before you head off into the real world of foreclosing buying.

We suggest you read the chapters in the first section in order, at least your first time through (of course you'll read it again!). You could skip the first section if you think you already know it all, but you'd miss some good stories. And we learned some very good lessons from our disasters. Since the adventure begins in the second section, you can read those topics as you work your way through the foreclosure auction process. The last section is like dessert. We'll let you decide whether to eat dessert first, but we may judge you for it.

Maybe you're interested in buying a fix-and-flip. Maybe you're looking at a buy-and-hold, either as an investment to rent or a home to own and live in yourself. Whatever your goal in buying real estate, the best way to make your money go furthest is to get it at a discount. And one of the main ways to do that is through foreclosures. But there is risk that's unique to buying a foreclosure, and that's what we want to help you mitigate. We're going to share the lessons we've learned from buying hundreds of foreclosures so that you can maximize your chances of success when it's your turn.

Let the adventure begin!

SECTION I
THE RULES OF THE GAME

CHAPTER 1

THE STARTING LIEN

A house for $200. It sounds ridiculous. When we tell people that we bought a house for $200, they don't believe us. They think we're making it up. But we actually did. It is possible. We know because we bought one. And no, it wasn't a complete tear-down. And it wasn't in the middle of nowhere. It was a cute little two-family house built in 1927 not too far from us in Massachusetts. We still own it to this day, and it generates $500 a month in free cash flow for us.

How did we do it, you might ask? A foreclosure auction.

So how do foreclosure auctions work? You show up, you get a full tour of a vacant property. They tell you all the things that are wrong with it.

Just kidding. No, they don't. They don't tell you jack. Maybe 5% of the time you're lucky enough to get access to the property before the auction. For the most part, you're just like everyone else twiddling your thumbs outside the house. Maybe you're not even allowed to stand on the property because the owner's there with a shotgun ("say hello to my little friend"). So the truth is you are literally buying a house sight unseen. You're basically bidding on a big mystery box.

Who does that? Crazy people do that. We do that. And you might be doing that. Because you can get some amazing deals at auction. Whether you're looking for a fix-and-flip or a property to buy-and-hold, either as a rental or as your own house, we think one of the best ways to get a deal in real estate is foreclosure. Whether you want to acquire a property to make money or to live in, you want to find a deal. In our experience, buying properties at foreclosure auctions is one of the very best ways to acquire great properties at a discount to market value.

That said, buying foreclosures isn't easy. To be 100% honest, we thought it was going to be a lot easier when we started out. At the time we didn't know what we didn't know. We've been investing in real estate for more than fifteen years now. We've bought literally hundreds of properties at foreclosure auctions and maybe two houses off the MLS. In fact, we both live in houses that we acquired in foreclosure. We've also built a great business that allows us to make an excellent living and gives us the time and freedom to do what we like.

So this is Kev's version of how we met: We were both in college at UMass. Back in the day, UMass had a really cool program where they would let students get credit by instructing phys ed classes. Kevin was pretty amazing in the world of Tae Kwon Do back in the day. Let's just say the Karate Kid got all the fame, but Kevin was a legend (in his own mind). And Matt is one of the weirdest guys you're ever going to meet. He'll try anything twice. But he was getting sick of being picked on for his long hair and ridiculous mullet, so he enrolled in Kevin's self-defense class.

That's Kev's version anyway. Matt says this is not how it happened. But however it actually happened, we became friends—probably because of a lack of options.

One day after we graduated, Kev was complaining about working for other people and making them much more financially successful than he was. He'd worked in a variety of sales roles—sales, sales management, sales team development, etc.—but he was growing dissatisfied. If he did a really great job, he might have a good month in terms of his paycheck, but the boss or the company had a GREAT month. Matt kept trying to convince Kev to invest in real estate. At first Kev wasn't convinced because that sounded like something adults do, and he wasn't sure he was adult enough yet. Actually, he's still not sure.

But Matt was like, "Let's do this and we'll work our way out of the rat race. Otherwise we're always going to be punching a clock somewhere and working for someone else. We're always going to make somebody else more successful than we're going to make ourselves unless we do this. If we get into real estate, we can grow our own business." So that was the origin of the idea, shifting our time away from working for someone else and toward making ourselves successful together. Eventually Matt got Kev to cave, and that's how we got started in real estate together.

By that time, Matt had already gotten his start in real estate. He bought his first duplex when he was sixteen with money he borrowed from his grandmother. He sold it when he was eighteen and made about $20k, which gave him a taste for real estate. Then right before meeting Kev, he bought a four-family building in Saginaw, Michigan, with his younger brother. At the time it seemed like a good deal. After Matt flew out from Massachusetts to see the property, flew home, and ran all the numbers, it seemed like it would cash flow. And it did, until the property manager started stealing from him. So Matt fired that property manager and hired a bigger company that ended up mismanaging it as well. It went more than 50% vacant for several months, and the last tenant who left stole everything of value from the property. The final blow was when the insurance company denied the claim for the loss because the building had been more than 50% vacant for more than three months. At that point the losses were just too big to absorb, and the property went into foreclosure. But even with that experience, Matt was hooked on real estate.

By the time we met, he was ready to try it again. He'd actually been let go from a job as a personal assistant for a wealthy lady in Amherst. So this time he dove in with both feet, building a network so that he could learn from other real estate professionals. One was a realtor who specialized in properties owned by the banks that had taken them back in foreclosure or REOs. Around that time in 2008, the market for REOs and foreclosures was really picking up. Matty started to see more and more distressed properties, especially in Springfield. There was just property after property boarded up across the city.

It turned out to be a great time for us to get into the market, because we knew we didn't want to pay full price for a turn-key property. We found a Boston-style duplex REO. Matt looked at it and the numbers seemed to work. We were excited to get into it with the $15k we'd saved up at the time along with money we leveraged from a hard money lender Kev had found. And then we basically rolled up our sleeves. Matt worked on the house during the day while Kevin was at his job. Matt was out there sanding the floors, and then Kevin would come in after work, change his clothes and help paint the walls—whatever we had to do. As we were renovating it, we had a lot of interested people walking by, "Oh, I wanna rent it! Let me rent it!" We just took the first person who came along. We refinanced the property after we had a tenant in there a couple months, paid off the hard money loan, and made a little cash profit, which we took and rolled it into the next property.

As an aside, that was our worst tenant ever *by far*. We learned that you don't just take the first person who comes along screaming, "Pick me! Pick me!" Now we're a little choosier about our tenants—but more on that in another book.

OH! OH! REO!

There's definitely a strategy for getting the best deal when buying REOs, and that's learning to network with REO agents. While some real estate agents might occasionally have one or two REO listings, the best agents are the ones the banks go to when they want to sell these properties fast. There's at least one REO specialist in almost every real estate market, and that's the person to work with.

Another way to get an inside track on the REO market is to become a service agent for the bank. Service agents work for the bank to secure the foreclosed properties they've taken back from auction. They perform lock changes. They may winterize the properties. We worked as a service-agent company for a time, and we got a lot of inside knowledge on how the banks conduct their REOs. We were also able to talk to the asset managers and the REO agents directly, so that gave us another leg-up on everyone else because we got into most of the properties before they were listed for sale publicly. So we could put in offers ahead of time, like a pocket listing.

For more info on buying REO properties, visit our YouTube channel, "Two Guys Take on Real Estate."

It was kind of just a domino effect after that, for the most part. We were basically using the BRRRR strategy—Buy, Rehab, Rent, Refinance, Repeat—before that term was coined. We still own that first house we bought. About three months later we bought our second house, a three-family that we own to this day, and our third house a couple months after that. By the end of our first year in business together, we'd bought twenty units. Within a couple of years, we were both working full-time for ourselves.

After that, we never looked back. We did whatever it took to make our business successful. We put all the hours in, sometimes practically sleeping at the properties we were renovating. We just worked hard and did whatever needed to be done at whatever project was in process. Matt looked at properties every week, hundreds of properties, and then he'd go back to work on the project. And he was learning as he went because he didn't have trade skills at the time. YouTube was our friend.

Eventually Matt got his general contractor's license. He met a lead inspector who took Matt under his wing. So he learned about de-leading and got licensed for it, because that was a big thing in Massachusetts. Almost every single home we ever bought either did not have lead remediation or it was not properly done, what's called "illegal de-leading." When we took a property on, we wanted to make sure it was safe, so we would go through and de-lead it.

Still, we stayed away from the foreclosure auction process until 2012. Looking back that probably was not smart, but we didn't know what we didn't know. We probably would have gotten a lot more deals if we'd started buying properties at foreclosure auctions earlier. We didn't have a process. We didn't have a team. We knew we could buy these properties and we could add value, but there were so many unknowns. Matt didn't yet have his contractor's license, and it's not like he had a construction background—he'd studied pre-med!

And the fact is, buying a property at a foreclosure auction was *scary*. We couldn't get inside the property before the auction. What if we were off on our renovation budget because we didn't anticipate all the issues? So we stayed away from foreclosures early on. But as the years progressed, we got a lot more knowledge. We also had more money and more properties that could offset a loss, so it was less risky.

And then there was the time we had to foreclose on a property ourselves.

OUR FIRST FORECLOSURE

When we first started out in business together, we brought in a partner who said he had a lot of experience. We brought him in at the same time we brought in another partner who had money. It seemed like a good idea at the time.

We knew business partners often put properties in their own names rather than the business's name, so they can access borrowing vehicles like FHA loans that are available only to individuals and that offer the maximum loan-to-value for a mortgage. It's a way to maximize the business's available capital for real estate investments. So we put some of the properties in our new partner's name.

Then he screwed us. He started stealing money out of our bank account. He basically took two properties for himself. He just said, "Nope, they're mine. They're in my name. They're not yours." We were like, "You knew what we were doing when we put them in your name! That was a business strategy. We weren't just giving them to you." It didn't matter. We were screwed.

Luckily, we had put the mortgage on them. We were the bank. So to get the properties back, we had to foreclose on our now-former partner. We had to hire a lawyer. We had to put public notice ads in the newspaper announcing the auction. It cost us $30k. It took us two years to complete the whole process—which is another reason we were scared away from foreclosures. But we got our houses back.

We also got an inside perspective on the process. And we became friends with the auctioneer, Corey. One day after our foreclosure was finished, Corey said to us, "Guys, you want to show up at this house. You should be there for the auction." He didn't tell us what the minimum bid was or any of the details, but when an auctioneer tells you that you should show up at an auction, it's a sign there's a deal to be had. So we showed up and got a fantastic deal.

Then we were like, "Wait a minute, how have we not been doing this before? We were scared about all the risks of buying houses at foreclosure auctions, but we just got a fantastic deal."

We bought it for about $25k, and we put in around $30k to renovate it. When it then appraised for $180k, we refinanced it for $100k—which is nearly $50k more than we put into it. So then we had $100k to buy more houses. At that point, we knew, "Oh my God. We need to go to more foreclosures. Let's put a system in place so that we can hit as many as possible."

So we did.

We still own that property and rent it out, and it is still cash flowing for us.

Ever since our first foreclosure, foreclosures have been one of the most consistent ways we've found deals. You can sometimes find a deal on the MLS or Zillow, but it's rare. Going to foreclosure auctions, you have a much better chance of finding a deal. You might have to go to multiple foreclosure auctions, but you still have a better chance of finding a property for below market value if you know how and you're diligent. Banks are usually looking to liquidate these properties and get them off their books quickly. They're not in the business of managing real estate; they're in the business of lending on it—which means there's almost always a market for foreclosures.

We regularly buy property for tens or even thousands of dollars less than market value, and we consistently find amazing deals. In the last seven years—even 2021 and 2022 when the mainstream housing market was going bananas—Matt was the only bidder who showed up to 30% of the foreclosure auctions he attended. We didn't win all those properties because most of the time the bank still wanted way more than we were willing to pay, but that fact gives you a sense of the opportunity. And it includes all kinds of property: single-family, multifamily, apartment buildings, condos, shopping centers, self-storage, any type of commercial property, vacant land. Anything that a bank would lend on has the potential to be foreclosed on. While we invest mostly in residential properties, and that's what we'll focus on here, you can apply the same principles to almost any type of real estate foreclosure.

A lot of people assume foreclosures are mostly distressed properties, or properties in need of significant repair. Some foreclosures are distressed, but not all. Not by a long shot. It might surprise people that more than 50% of the properties we see at auction are in move-in ready condition. Some foreclosures are occupied, and if they're occupied then they're generally habitable. They might need some repair and some updating, but usually the people living in a property don't want to destroy it. We've bought houses at foreclosure that we didn't do any work on and then turned around and sold at a $60k profit.

If you're new to foreclosure buying or if your goal is a house that's not a major rehab and you're just looking for a deal, you can find it. Especially if you're a buyer looking for your own home, you can find a really good deal. A homebuyer can always pay more at a foreclosure auction than an investor because investors need to make a profit, whereas homebuyers are usually just looking for a deal relative to the mainstream real estate market. And you can find them in any neighborhood at any price point. We've bought multimillion-dollar houses, although you're typically going to see those less often than foreclosures on houses in the $25k-$450k range.

We've heard a lot in the past several years about how investors—you know, people partnering up and creating LLCs, evil companies, and private equity firms—have been buying up properties so that regular, good, single-family homebuyers couldn't find a home they could afford. Investors like us were driving up prices, that was the buzz. Ironically, the opposite happened for us. When it comes to buying property at foreclosure auctions, a regular homeowner looking to buy a place to live will always outbid us by far. In the foreclosure market, investors aren't driving up the price. If anything, all the people looking for a regular house to live in themselves have driven up the prices of houses in foreclosure to where investors aren't winning them all anymore.

Maybe you're thinking, "Gosh, I'll never bother going to a foreclosure auction. Why would I bother? All these big, mean corporations are out there bidding up the prices." To you, we'd say, "Are you kidding? Go to the foreclosure auctions! These corporate guys are never going to touch what you're able to offer in price. You're the one offering way more than they'd be willing to spend." Use it to your advantage! Just know what you're doing first.

DISTRESSED FOR SUCCESS

An investor can add different types of value to a property. One clear value-add is putting a new roof on the property or updating the kitchen and bath. Another value-add is putting in a good management company, updating leases, and getting market-rent tenants. Because of how the market has shifted in recent years, "distressed property" has taken on a different meaning. "Distressed" doesn't necessarily mean "run-down." It may just mean there's an opportunity to increase its value in any number of ways.

We recently got a deal under contract for $6.5 million on a multifamily property that we considered distressed. The property is in good shape, but all the rents are depressed relative to the market. Until we bought it, a mom-and-pop operation ran the property. The dad bought it years ago, then left it to two sons who are now in their seventies and looking to exit. Because they owed nothing on it, they were fine keeping rents below-market. It meant that people complained less about the condition of their units.

Because there are no active leases, we can now renegotiate terms with the tenants while trying to keep as many as possible. Because the property has a lot of units, it will take us six months to a year to get everyone on a lease that is closer to market rent. The tenants will also have a better management company that's more responsive. The previous owners did a pretty good job, but they didn't have a maintenance staff. For instance, one of the residents was a plumber who pitched in on the building during his off-hours. Now if we get a maintenance call, we'll get a plumber on-site in an hour.

For more information on buying distressed property and unlocking hidden value, visit our YouTube channel, "Two Guys Take on Real Estate."

The foreclosure market is tied to the economic cycle. When the economy is strong, you see fewer foreclosures. When the economy is in recession, you see more. Inflation can have a huge impact on the foreclosure market because property values tend to go up drastically. Then property taxes and homeowners' insurance go up drastically. The cost of water, the cost of repairs, the cost of the labor, all that goes up due to inflation. That could be the downfall of a housing market and obviously the rest of the markets. People end up having less savings; often there are job losses in an economy experiencing high inflation.

Then you might see an uptick in bank foreclosures among working-class people who bought houses as costs rose drastically. Maybe they end up losing their jobs, and then they can't afford the house they just stretched to buy. If home prices fall due to the lower demand when interest rates rise, people can't sell out of the homes they can't afford. They're kind of stuck. If they can't afford the mortgage and they can't sell the property, they may end up in foreclosure.

That's when you might get a real bargain at a foreclosure auction, like our $200 house.

THE $200 HOUSE

Matt got to the house on the day of the auction and did a full walkthrough around the outside—which is typical because most of the time you can't get inside before the auction. Based on the condition of the property that he could see and the calculations that he ran on the ARV, or "after repair value," and the rehab costs, he was ready to bid up to $50k. Then the auctioneer opened the bidding at "one hundred."

Matt's first thought was that we were out of luck, because the opening bid was already higher than our maximum bid. But that's not what the auctioneer meant. She meant "one hundred dollars." Once he realized that, Matt tried to bid $101. Because he's that cheap. Sadly, the auctioneer wouldn't let him. So he offered $200—and won. We still had to write a deposit check for $5,000, so when the deal closed we got a refund check for $4,800. We then turned around and sold the property to one of our contractors for $79k, who renovated it and sold it back to us for $180,000. We still own it to this day, and it generates $500 a month for us in free cash flow.

So while you can get an amazing deal, you really have to prepare yourself for all the things that could go wrong. We've been to auctions where people were bidding on a house that was occupied, and we could hear them talking amongst themselves, "Well, the people are going to be gone when we buy it, right?" They were bidding on a house when they had no idea that dealing with occupants is a huge component in foreclosures that can prolong the holding period and result in major costs. We've seen people get themselves into risky situations because they think, "Hey, I'll just buy a cheap house. It's going to be super easy."

Most of the time, there are red flags you should notice when you're at a foreclosure auction. For instance, one of the big things: underground oil tanks. If you're not getting inside and you don't inspect the outside, how do you know that there isn't an underground oil tank on the property? Maybe you don't even know what an underground oil tank is. Well, someone a long time ago had the brilliant idea of burying a giant tank made of metal and filling it with oil. And why not? What could possibly go wrong? It's not like metal rusts or anything, and even if it did, it's not like the EPA would have an issue with it.

By now we hope you're thinking, "You've gotta be kidding! That's a major problem." Yes, we're kidding and oh, yes, it's a major problem. So if you take over a house with an underground oil tank, even if you didn't know about it when you bought it, it's basically a game-over scenario for you and your investors. It could wipe out your entire investment. If the tank is leaking and the oil is leaching into the groundwater, you're in BIG trouble.

There are a few other red flags you should be concerned about. Lead paint, for instance, can require expensive remediation, especially if you're planning to rent the property. Asbestos is another risk. In New England we run across "snowmen," boilers installed eighty to one hundred years ago that were later sprayed with asbestos to make them more efficient, so now they're all white. Another example is knob and tube electrical wiring—which was state of the art in 1880. It's a red flag for insurance companies and can be hard to discover if the house has a new meter on the outside but an old junction box that connects to the old wiring on the inside where you can't see it. If you notice any of these issues on a property during your due diligence, you might want to stay away from it. The best foreclosure may be the one you don't bid on.

Keep in mind, though, that you won't be able to see these issues most of the time because you rarely have access inside the property before the auction. You often have to make judgment calls about a property based on what you can see. If the siding looks to be seventy years old, you can guess that the heating system is about the same age too. What if people are camping outside the house? It could be a nightmare, or it could be an amazing opportunity. Kevin loves it when we score an occupied foreclosure property because he knows that we got it for way less than anybody else could have, because other buyers will run the other way if there's an occupant. If you have a process for dealing with occupants, whether they're the former owners or bona fide tenants or just squatters stealing the copper pipes, if you have a good process for addressing these problems or any of the red flag concerns, then you have the ability to really score yourself a deal. But you need to be sure you put a process in place before you bid.

Especially if you're new to buying foreclosures and you don't have that process in place and you're just buying a property because you're excited about getting a $200 house like we did, you're following a recipe for disaster. We've seen it time and time again, so many noobs basically getting crushed. Matt was at an auction not long ago for a two-family house. Nobody could get inside before the auction. This other guy bid the price way up. Then we got into it after the fact: no kitchen, no plumbing, asbestos in the basement. The winning bidder had to walk away from his $5k deposit, which was the smart thing to do because otherwise he'd be in for a loss many times that amount.

We learned this lesson the expensive way.

OUR WORST DEAL EVER

Back in 2016 we bought a foreclosure in central Connecticut, about two hours from where we live. Connecticut is a judicial state (we'll explain more about judicial states and nonjudicial states in Chapter 2 and Chapter 6), and we found the property through the court website. Especially in Connecticut, you can go onto the court database, look up the property, and read the appraisal report. You can read what's called the foreclosure worksheet. You can see outstanding liens, debt, stuff like that, so you can get a really good sense of what is going on with the property. At the time we were still looking at the Zillow values of properties to help establish our ARV. We don't rely on them anymore, but Zillow estimated the market value of the property at $1.1 million. So we used that as our ARV.

All foreclosure auctions across Connecticut happen on Saturday at high noon. So on the Saturday of the auction, we drove nearly two hours to the property. When we got there, we learned the opening bid would be $250k. We also got an appraisal report, so we knew the house was in rough shape. Then we were able to get inside.

It was LARGE. The people in the town had actually nicknamed it "The Fortress." It was built in the '70s by an architect for his family. When you think "architect-designed house," you think extravagant and unique—which adds to the complexity of a rehab. We could see clearly that pipes had burst. The roof was leaking. There was lots and lots of glass, and most of it was broken and needed to be replaced. The sliders were all broken. The floor had radiant heat, and the pipes underneath it had burst. That meant we'd have to jackhammer the floors out to repair the pipes. There was even a pool in the center of the house that needed to be repaired.

It would be a lot of work. Still, being naïve, we thought that the spread between the opening bid of $250k and our ARV of $1.1M was wide. Even if we had to spend $300k on the rehab, there would be plenty of room to make out like bandits. So we came up with the number we were willing to bid based on our rehab budget and what we assumed for the ARV.

The required deposit was set at $80k, which is a high number for a foreclosure. High deposits like that typically weed out some of the competition because not everyone can afford to plop down eighty grand and wait several months for the foreclosure to process before they get access to the property. Two other bidders showed up. Even the bank showed up. The bank doesn't always attend the auction, but this time they were there.

And then we won it, for around $400k. We were all excited. One of our partners was already counting his chickens before they hatched, "We're each making a couple hundred thousand dollars in profit!" It was pretty exciting.

The appraisal on it was around $700k as is, so we'd won it for much less than the appraisal. With Connecticut being a judicial state, our winning bid still had to be approved by a judge. And because our bid was so much lower than the appraised amount, the judge considered sending the property back to auction again. The court was concerned that the bidding wasn't fair to the owner since the owner would receive any excess proceeds after the bank lien was paid off. In other words, the higher the winning bid, the more the owner stood to recover. We had to convince the judge that the house was worth much less than the appraisal by going back to the house, taking pictures of the condition, and presenting our case. It took months for the judge to review the deal. Unfortunately, in judicial states the closing doesn't always happen in thirty or sixty days; it could be months and months.

All the time that the court was reviewing our bid, we didn't have access to the $80k deposit—earning no interest and with no guarantee that the house would be ours. If the judge didn't approve the deal, we would be out five months of opportunity on $80,000. We'd also be out the money we spent on property insurance. As soon as we win a bid, even before the deal closes, we have an insurable interest in the property. Foreclosure auctions are "as is, where is." That means that if the house burns to the ground the day after the auction, we're still on the hook to close the deal or else lose our deposit. We didn't want to risk losing an $80k deposit, so we paid $3k for an insurance policy.

After five months, the judge finally approved our bid. The house was ours! At last we could send our crew down to the property, along with ten thirty-yard dumpsters.

Once we emptied the place of mountains of trash, we got a better view of what was really going on—and it was even worse than we thought. There was a lot more damage than we could see before. There were splits in the plumbing. We had to replace the entire roof. And there was mold.

Because the rehab was bigger than we expected, we started calling local contractors and learned that they were much pricier in that part of Connecticut than they were where we lived in Massachusetts. The prices were two or three times what we normally paid on our rehabs. And since the scope of work had already blown up, we decided to send our contractors down there instead. That meant we would lose our ability to get other jobs done closer to home. We also put them up in hotel rooms for a week or two at a time. It was expensive and it ate into our budget, but it was still cheaper than hiring locally.

Matt was also going down there at least once a week, which isn't as often as he usually visits big projects. But he lost a full day every time he went to the property because he spent four hours in the car just driving there and back. He couldn't afford the time away from our projects nearer home. Managing the project was very difficult without a local team to rely on. With the crew traveling back and forth and Matt traveling back and forth, the project timeline got pushed farther and farther back. The crew ran into one issue after the next, because the house was so odd.

That's when the brand-new roof started to leak. When we filed the insurance claim, the insurance company denied it on the grounds that one of the few local contractors we hired wasn't covered for the particular type of roof he installed. So we had to pay for the repair out of our own pockets.

Every day our budget was blowing up more and more and more. Meanwhile the holding costs were eating us alive: our hard money loan at 10%, property taxes, oil for the heat since by now it was winter. We were paying to heat the place and couldn't even be there on a consistent basis. Without a local team to keep an eye on the property, a pipe burst right after we replaced the plumbing. We came back after the holidays and all the windows were coated in ice. The house was one big frozen frickin' Popsicle. So then the heating system was shot. We fought with the insurance company over that claim too, which took months and months.

In the meantime, we had to make the repairs and keep going. We again tried to find contractors locally to put in a new heating system, and they just kept taking advantage of the terrible situation we were in. It was a mess. We kept thinking, "We've got to keep going so we can sell this property as quickly as possible." We tried selling it "as is" to some local contractors who could finish it, and they all low-balled us with their offers. They knew we were in a bad position. They offered us less than we paid for the property even after we'd put $200k of rehab into it. We couldn't eat that loss. Eventually another business partner had a brilliant idea and found a couple who wanted to buy it as their home even though it wasn't yet finished.

We agreed that they would buy it while it was still under renovation and then we would finish it to a certain point. It seemed like a perfect solution at the time, but it turned out to be one of our biggest mistakes. We will never do that again. The buyers' expectations of our work and our plan for the house did not match. We're investors who flip houses. They were first-time homebuyers who expected a custom home. We ended up arguing about everything. Even after we'd sold it, we were still funneling money into it and sending our employees down to the property to do more work than we'd bargained for. The opportunity cost was huge, because we didn't have our guys available locally to make us money on all our other properties.

Then the new owners sued us. The legal wrangling took years. The original idea was that the sale would stop the bleeding for us, but it just added more fuel to the fire.

Even before the lawsuit, we lost about $300k. So what did we learn?

We now limit the geographic area of the properties we buy to within about an hour of home, and ideally closer. Unless we know that there's really good profit and it's a cream puff, not a big rehab, we stay away. If we're going to buy a property farther out than that, we get local boots on the ground. We lose too much opportunity sending our crew to far-flung properties. We have a good system where we are. We know what we're doing where we are. We can make money where we are. If we keep taking our team off task locally, it costs us more than we could gain.

Also, we will never again sell a property before the rehab is complete. We're just never going to meet homeowner expectations. We are not custom homebuilders. When we buy a house to sell it, our strategy is to fix and flip. We'd rather show a finished product, and we do the same with our rentals. We'd rather show prospective buyers and tenants, "This is what you're getting. Don't expect granite here if you're seeing laminate." We learned about setting expectations a long time ago. We'll never forget it again.

Two more lessons we learned from this deal: 1) have multiple exit strategies, and 2) be willing to cut your losses. When we first realized that the scope was much bigger than we anticipated, we should have sold the property as is. Even before we started the rehab, we had the opportunity to sell it. We reached out to the other bidders at the auction, and they were willing to buy it from us. If we'd taken their offer, we would have lost $80k instead of $300k-plus.

Next, if you don't have the workforce to do rehab that's needed on the foreclosure you buy, don't buy that property. If your due diligence shows you that the property needs a lot of rehab, make sure you have the people to do the work on the timeline and budget you need. If you don't have the workforce to make that happen, don't buy that property or only buy it for a song so that you're cool with sitting on it.

And make sure you perform proper due diligence on your contractors. We definitely read the insurance policies for the contractors we hire a little bit more thoroughly. They may tell you, "Yeah, I do rubber roofing." That doesn't mean they are insured for rubber roofing. Talk to their insurance agent, talk to your insurance agent. If you don't know how to read an insurance policy, have your insurance broker read their policy. And make sure you get added as an additional insured so you are covered for the work the contractor performs for you and so that the insurance company will pay you out in case of a claim.

We've learned a lot of lessons in fifteen years of buying foreclosed properties. That's why we can be brutally honest about what you might find. It's also why we can teach you not to make the mistakes we've made. Remember that if you have good processes and procedures to handle the potential pitfalls, then foreclosed property could be a gold mine.

Even if you've never bought property before, buying a foreclosure could be an excellent way to kick off a real estate investment strategy because you can walk away with a great, underpriced property. Obviously, there is less risk buying a property that you can thoroughly walk through with a home inspector. That approach is less risky, but the returns are also a lot less. If you're buying a house like our $200 house, then for the most part there's no way in heck you could lose. Even if you have to demo it and sell the property as an undeveloped lot, in most cities and towns in this country it's still worth at least $20k.

Particularly if your goal is to acquire a rental property, buying below market value reduces your risk. There are so many unknowns with rental property, especially in tenant-friendly states like Massachusetts where landlords get sued all the time. Paying a lower price-per-unit is a massive risk mitigator. We once bought a portfolio at $18k per unit from an owner looking to liquidate. Before we completed the renovation and got the property fully rented, there were so many costly hiccups along the way. But because we bought the property cheaply, we were protected from loss. If we'd bought the same portfolio at $50k per unit, the hiccups would probably have killed our business. Knowing from experience that cheaper is better, we've made buying property at foreclosure auctions a cornerstone of our strategy.

We know a guy who used to be a Massachusetts state policeman. A few years ago, he started showing up at foreclosure auctions in our area. He wasn't looking for his personal house; he focused on buying rental property and building a rental portfolio. First he was working full-time while attending auctions in his spare time, then he was working part-time and the rest of the time he'd go to auctions and find deals. Then he left his day job. Now he's retired from the state police and he's a full-time real estate investor. Like 90% of wealthy people in this country, he secured his financial freedom by investing in real estate— and he did it buying foreclosures.

We learned how to do it. He learned how to do it. You can learn how to do it too.

THE TWO GUYS TAKE ON FORECLOSURE AUCTIONS

- Buying properties at foreclosure auctions is one of the very best ways to acquire great properties at a discount to market value, but it is not for the faint of heart.

- Banks are usually looking to get foreclosed properties off their books quickly. They're not in the business of managing real estate; they're in the business of lending on it—which means there's almost always a market for foreclosures.

- A lot of people assume foreclosures are mostly distressed properties, but in fact more than 50% of the properties we see at auction are in move-in-ready condition.

- A homebuyer can always pay more at a foreclosure auction than an investor because investors need to make a profit, whereas homebuyers are usually just looking for a deal relative to the mainstream real estate market.

- While you can get an amazing deal, you really have to prepare yourself for all the things that could go wrong.

CHAPTER 2

KNOW BEFORE YOU GO

Let's talk about what it means to buy a foreclosure.

Yes, you're buying a property that someone else has lost. They owe a debt, and there's a lien on the property because of that debt. Sometimes the owner just fell on hard times. They got behind on the mortgage, the bank imposed late fees, the overdue balance built up, and they just couldn't dig out of the hole. Often people haven't paid the mortgage for years. Or maybe the property taxes or the condo association fees got to be more than they could afford. We understand how it happens all too well because it actually happened to Matt with that rental property in Michigan. And now whoever holds the debt has given up on ever collecting the money from the property owner, so they're foreclosing and holding an auction to get their money back.

Most of the properties we buy are vacant. By the time the foreclosure happens, often the owner has already cut ties with it. If people are still living there, we work with them in a way that the banks won't to help smooth the transition to a new living situation. We're usually very willing to negotiate to make the process easier. We'll give them more time to move out. We even help them move. We may rent the property back to them as landlords, which frees them up from the often-expensive responsibility of being a property owner. We've even sold houses back to the occupants for more than we paid but less than they previously owed, which was a real win-win for everyone.

If a property doesn't sell to a bidder at the foreclosure auction, then it becomes an REO. Without investors or other buyers stepping in, places with a lot of foreclosures—like our hometown of Springfield fifteen years ago—can become blighted areas. In Springfield, they consistently had a problem with fires in vacant homes, likely as a result of vagrants and drug addicts using empty buildings for shelter. So when that happens, then the property is endangering other people, and also lowering the value of all the other homes around it. When banks are in charge of properties, they aren't known for being the most on top of maintenance or landscaping or any of the general upkeep. They've definitely gotten better in recent years because they got slapped around a lot by local governments after 2008. But still, big banks are not positioned to own real estate. They're positioned to lend on real estate.

The result of a failed foreclosure auction becoming an REO is often even worse for the property owner. At that point, the owner is dealing with the bank, which then recruits its army of lawyers to initiate the eviction process. The bank is usually a big corporation with high-powered lawyers, and they're not going to play around. They're simply going to move the eviction through the process as quickly as possible. Where a bank will just evict the owners in an assembly-line process, we can be more flexible. While our goal is to acquire the property and make money, we can also do a little good by working with the former owners.

So what exactly is a "foreclosure"? Essentially, a property owner has a bill they're legally obligated to pay, which is secured by the property, whether it be a tax bill, a mortgage bill, or a condo association fee bill. A limited number and type of debts can result in a lien and lead to a foreclosure on a property. Generally, unpaid mortgage debts, property taxes, and homeowners' association and condo association fees can result in a lien that could produce a foreclosure. Other liens can be attached to a property that generally don't result in a foreclosure, such as mechanic's liens and most federal tax liens.

After a certain amount of time, the entity that is owed money puts a lien on the property and becomes a "lienholder." After more time and effort to collect payment on the bill, the lienholder starts a legal process to recover what they're owed by liquidating the property that secures the loan. That legal process is called a foreclosure. First the lienholder will issue the property owner a notice that the owner is in default and give them a specified amount of time to "cure" the default by paying the debt. If the property owner does not pay the debt within the specific time, then the lienholder issues a public notice of foreclosure. After a period of time that's usually dictated by state law, the lienholder puts the property up for sale at a foreclosure auction.

The entire process is often lengthy, years rather than months. Usually many months of nonpayment by the property owner pass before a lienholder starts the foreclosure process. Even after the process is well underway, the property owner can often still cure the default and keep the property. In many states, the property owner has until the very last hour before a foreclosure auction to pay the debt and stop the process. Where we live in Massachusetts, the process often takes a year or two. We were involved in one foreclosure where the bank waited ten years before selling the property at a foreclosure auction, and the homeowner lived in the house without paying the mortgage the entire time.

When we talk about foreclosure investing on social media, there's a lot of empathy toward the poor homeowner who's losing their home and the families being uprooted: "They're going to go homeless! How could anybody want to profit from that situation?"

Those people generally pull back in their positions once they understand a little bit more about how a foreclosure auction happens. Everybody understands that life happens. People fall behind on their debts. You change jobs. You have an illness. You get a month or two or even six behind on your mortgage. That's a different thing. And the banks bend over *backward* to work with you generally when that happens. The last thing the banks want to do is repossess a home. A car dealer doesn't want to repossess your old Chevy and then try to auction it— unless it happens to be a 1970 Chevy Chevelle SS 454. They're going to lose money, just like a landlord doesn't want to evict somebody for nonpayment. It's usually a last-ditch effort to recoup a loss when the person involved has shown that they're really not open to working out a solution or doing the right thing. Critics start pulling their positions back when they begin to understand that many of these foreclosures result after years and years of nonpayment. And in the meantime, the house has been run into the ground and the city hasn't been paid for property taxes—which we all need to fund our schools and libraries and first responders.

Critics start pulling back when they realize, "Wait a second. These people borrowed money from a local bank that my cousin works at. Now my cousin got laid off because that bank got screwed. These people aren't doing their part in society at all, and everybody else has to pay more taxes to offset *their* unpaid taxes. These guys aren't paying their fair share!" We get it that life happens, and sometimes people hit a stumbling block. But by the time a foreclosure auction comes around, there have been years of stumbling blocks. The owner made bad decisions, they didn't just have bad luck. So there are definitely people like, "Wow, don't you think about the poor people involved?" And we're like, "Yeah, but that only goes so far until you see the entire picture."

THE EIGHT-YEAR FORECLOSURE

We bought a nice house with a pool on a corner lot at a foreclosure auction, knowing it was clearly occupied. We've dealt with this situation quite a bit, so we have a process for dealing with the occupants, and we budget for the anticipated costs. We generally expect that the process will take six months.

The occupant (we'll call her "C") and her husband had lived in the house for years. C's husband was the mortgage holder, and after he passed away in 2013, C stopped paying the mortgage. By the time of the foreclosure, C was living in the house with her adult daughter along with her daughter's boyfriend and their child. None of the three adult occupants paid the mortgage while they lived in the house for years after the husband's death. When the bank initiated the foreclosure process, C got a lawyer to defend her and successfully impeded the process. But eight years after C stopped paying the mortgage, the bank finally held a foreclosure auction right at the property.

When the deal closed and we became the legal owners of the property, Kev did what he normally does when we buy occupied property: He knocked on the door hoping to have a conversation with the occupant and begin negotiating their departure.

The conversation went the way it often goes. Kev found out that the occupants were related to the former owner. That meant they were not bona fide tenants with a valid lease in force. That meant they were squatting. And C claimed—bizarrely—that they had no idea the house had been sold in a foreclosure auction. She acted very surprised.

Kev typically starts these conversations acting a little surprised himself that a person is still living in a property we just bought, knowing full well that they don't own it anymore. So he met C's surprise with his own. When Kev asked what her plan was now that the house was sold and explained that the time had come for the family to move on, she gave him the usual spiel: "Oh, gosh, we had no idea that we were losing the house! We don't know what to do. This is all so unexpected. We'll have to talk to our lawyer, who was trying to resolve this situation with the bank. We can't believe this is happening! We'll have to look into it. Thanks for stopping by."

It was obvious to Kev that C was going to drag the situation out for as long as she could—which is totally typical. In the meantime, she was not going to budge. So Kev let her know that he needed to perform a safety inspection of the property and change all the locks, providing the occupants with new keys, of course. As the new owner, he needed to make sure the home was safe to live in because we're strictly liable for any harm that occurs on our property. C agreed to allow the safety inspection. Kev told her he'd be in touch soon to schedule it.

When we contacted C again to schedule the inspection, she refused. This time, she told Kev that she'd talked to an attorney who told her not to let anybody into the property for any reason. And then she started stonewalling. Kev tried several—many—more times to schedule the inspection, but she ignored him completely. We had no idea whether she was talking with an attorney or what she was doing. Finally, Kev told her he had no choice but to sue her for access to the property. Still no response. So Kev did exactly that: He took her to court. The judge agreed with us that it was fair and reasonable that a landlord have access to inspect the property, make sure it's safe, and install new locks.

Because we had to go to court, we were able to reestablish communication with C. Once again, Kev tried discussing her plans for moving the family out. He usually offers a bunch of different options to help in these situations, such as a few more days to get organized, a few thousand bucks to cover relocation expenses, a moving van or a dumpster to ease the actual moving process, those kinds of things. C admitted that the family had been able to save money because they'd had no housing expenses for nearly a decade. At that point, Kev said, "Awesome. I can help you out, and you also have money saved. It sounds like we'll be able to work this out."

Then he let C know that our plan for the property was to resell it and suggested that maybe we could sell it to her. Since her deceased husband was on the original deed and he was the one who was foreclosed on, her credit history hadn't been affected. Now there were three able-bodied, working adults living in the property. Perhaps one or more of them might qualify for a loan to buy it. We've negotiated this solution several times over the years. If it worked in this case, it would be a little silver lining in an otherwise stressful situation for all parties involved. We'd give them a pretty good deal, a little bit below market value, for a quick sale on a property they already live in.

C and her family were excited when Kev proposed the solution. They swore up and down that they were going to work with different banks to get approved for a mortgage loan.

Over the next several weeks, though, Kev couldn't get any hard answers from them. He even tried dropping by the house, but it was never a good time to discuss the plan for the sale. They clearly weren't making any progress, so we had to start the eviction.

The eviction process takes a long time in general, but by this time the pandemic eviction moratorium had kicked in. We had to pause the eviction as soon as we started it, and for about eleven months C didn't pay anything to live in the property. She wasn't even keeping the property up other than mowing the lawn. We were paying all the bills, including the bill for the water in their pool.

After nearly a year, we were able to resume the eviction process and still they wouldn't negotiate an end to the situation. Instead, they contested it by claiming they were victims throughout the entire foreclosure process. They claimed that the bank should never have foreclosed, even though it hadn't been paid on its loan in almost a decade. C alleged that the bank was the bad guy who had pursued an improper foreclosure and should never have held the auction. When that didn't work, she argued that her family should be allowed more time to move. We'd been willing to offer her time when the process started two years before that, but by this time our patience had run out. C argued that because the family had limited income, they should be allowed to stay in the house for $700 a month—well below market rent. That isn't how market value works! If you don't have a lot of money in your pocket, milk doesn't cost less at the store. But that's what she argued. Next she alleged that there were problems with the property like mold, because we didn't maintain it. We found that argument very ironic given their initial refusal to let us even inspect it.

It took thirteen months, but eventually we were able to get a court order of eviction. We contacted the sheriff's office to arrange for a deputy to be onsite to oversee it. But a few days before the big day, C filed an emergency motion to stop it. So once again we were back in court before the judge. This time C promised she would move her family, but renewed her claim that she needed more time in exchange for paying us a "reasonable" fee for use and occupancy. The judge issued an order giving C one more month in the house in exchange for $1,700, which was less than market value rent.

That fee didn't come close to covering our costs. In all, it cost us roughly $20k in holding costs for the two years that C lived in our property with her family without paying us anything. But it was a tiny victory that we were finally able to get C to cough up $1,700 for the very last month she was there.

C and her family lived for free on the bank's dime for almost eight years, and then lived basically for free on our dime for almost two years. We subsidized the lives of three able-bodied, working-class adults who lived rent-free for years. Even after all that, after having taken advantage of pretty much everybody who came into contact with them for as long as they could, the family continued to plead "victim." They've told their story to every news station that would listen and given interviews about how horrific their entire experience was at the hand of evil banks and heartless landlords.

All we can say in response is that they cost everybody around them a horrific amount of money to subsidize their lives for nearly a decade.

AS IS, WHERE IS

The terms of foreclosure auctions are typically "as is, where is," which means you're buying the property literally as you see it. But be warned: It *doesn't* mean "as you see it on the day of the foreclosure auction." It means "as you see it the day the sale closes," which may be months later. As of the day of the auction, the winning bidder has a legal obligation to buy the property from the lienholder at a later date when the deal closes. Whatever happens to the property between the date of the auction and the date the winning bidder closes on the property is the winning bidder's responsibility. The sale is still "as is, where is."

So if there's an occupant on the property, you're accepting it's going to have an occupant. If the property is a farm with cows and chickens and horses and a bull and all this other farm stuff on it, guess what? You're buying it with all that stuff. And if occupants move onto the property while you're waiting to close, it's still on you to deal with them after you close. Basically, you're buying a property sight-unseen and without any guarantees as to the condition of it. The sellers are not going to kick out the occupants or remove the garbage or fix the roof. They're not going to insure it. The buyer is not going to be able to conduct prepurchase inspections or perform a preoccupancy walk-through to assess whether it's in acceptable condition for closing. As the buyer, what you see on the day of the auction is (maybe) what you get when you close—unless it burns to the ground. In which case you'll get a burnt-down house.

If there's a car on there, yeah, you own it. But then there's a process for acquiring it because you have to get a title for a car. So there's a separate process you have to go through to actually acquire the title. But if there's other equipment, like a tractor, you would acquire it when you close. In the meantime if someone comes in and steals it, then you don't get the tractor. If there's plumbing in the house at the time of the auction and then sometime before you close someone steals it all, then you get a house with no plumbing.

At times we've gotten some valuable additional stuff. We've gotten mowers worth $3k and a few very nice antique tables. Kev once got a carload of wrapping paper. The time he took to haul it out of the house was probably worth more than the paper, but he was like, "Woo hoo! I'm set for Christmas for the next ten years!" Usually we let our crew pick through stuff when they're cleaning out the house. Many of them have furnished their whole homes that way. Matt's grandmother would've loved to pick through some of the houses when she was still around because she used to Google antique auctions online. We know we've thrown away stuff that she would have kept. "No! My God, that's worth a fortune." Kev actually thinks it's a lot of fun to "treasure-hunt" in an abandoned house. It's one of his guilty pleasures.

JUDICIAL V. NONJUDICIAL STATES

Every state handles foreclosures differently, so it's critical to know the laws and rules in the specific state where the property is located. One major factor that impacts the foreclosure process and therefore impacts foreclosure buyers is whether the state where the property is located is a "judicial foreclosure state" (like Connecticut) or a "nonjudicial foreclosure state" (like Massachusetts).

In judicial foreclosure states, foreclosures are administered by the state courts, which determine and oversee the entire process. A lienholder must petition the court and receive a judgment before proceeding with a foreclosure and holding a foreclosure auction. In addition, a judge must approve the winning auction bid. One convenient aspect of foreclosures in judicial states is that you can usually find information about upcoming foreclosure auctions on a state-maintained website.

A nonjudicial foreclosure state is basically just that: The foreclosure process isn't administered by the state, so it doesn't have to go through the courts first. Instead, the lienholder can simply file the proper paperwork and start the foreclosure process. In most nonjudicial states, lienholders use third-party auctioneers to conduct the auctions. Most, but not all, third-party auctioneers have websites where they post information about upcoming foreclosure auctions. Since information about upcoming foreclosure auctions isn't aggregated into a single convenient website, we use scrubbing software to pull the data from multiple websites into reports for us.

Often judicial states require higher deposits, so you have more money tied up in the property for some period of time. Other than that though, the cost of the process of acquiring a property is the same in both judicial and nonjudicial states. You do have attorney fees, but you're going to have attorney fees anyway. And we've often had a foreclosure contested at some point in the process in nonjudicial states, especially if the property is occupied.

Which is another upside with judicial states: The property is more likely to be vacant because the homeowner knows that the auction is the end of the road. In nonjudicial states, they just seem to dig their heads in the sand. They ignore the process for as long as possible, and as long as nobody is coming to their house or kicking them out, it doesn't seem real. Even by the time we win an auction in Massachusetts, it's not game over for the homeowner because they can still go to court and contest the foreclosure. Attorneys will take their cases and buy homeowners time with stall tactics. In Connecticut, the homeowner who wants to fight the foreclosure has exhausted almost all their options by the time the auction happens. They understand it's game over.

LIEN PRIORITY

Before you bid on a property in a foreclosure auction, it's important to understand "lien priority." There could be multiple liens on a property. Depending on which lienholder causes the foreclosure, other liens on the property may or may not be wiped out as a result of the foreclosure auction. Especially if the property is subject to a bank foreclosure, you need to know if there are multiple mortgages—first, second, third, and so on—and which one is foreclosing. You'll also have to research whether there are any tax, municipal, or additional mortgage liens as well. Otherwise you could be in for a nasty surprise.

If the property has a second mortgage that forecloses, for instance, it's possible that there could also be a first mortgage lien, a condo lien, a property tax lien and/or other municipal liens on the property as well. Property tax liens are always the highest priority. In some states, condominium owners' association (COA) and homeowners' association (HOA) liens are also super-priority liens. First mortgages are higher priority than second mortgages. If you acquire a property in a second-mortgage foreclosure auction, you could be on the hook to pay off all the other liens that are superior to the second mortgage or else lose your deposit.

While bank liens, tax liens, and COA/HOA liens are the most common, other less common liens could also exist on a property. It's important to understand the implications of these liens if they exist *before* bidding on a property at auction. For instance, federal liens attached to a property for nonpayment of income taxes typically include a 120-day right of redemption by the government. If there is a federal lien on the property, then the IRS or the federal agency that attached the lien has 120 days after the deal closes to enforce their lien and take the property. In our experience, they rarely do it—but it is a risk. If they do exercise their right, then they're required to pay the winning bidder only what the bidder paid at the auction. Typically if we acquire a property with a federal lien, we wait 120 days before we do any work. Otherwise, we could lose any money we put into the property over and above our bid.

Foreclosures generally do not result from mechanic's liens. Mechanic's liens are attached to a property as the result of a judgment against a homeowner for nonpayment of a contractor. In most cases, mechanic's liens get wiped out as the result of foreclosure auctions because they're so low on the totem pole of lien priority. But if somehow you acquire a property before the foreclosure process is complete, it's important to be aware the lien exists and to have a plan for curing the debt.

If you're not an expert in researching property titles and liens, our advice is to hire an attorney who specializes in real estate to do it for you.

THE HOUSE ON A LAKE

We were all excited about this house on a lake in western Massachusetts. Before the auction, we did our due diligence on back taxes and unpaid utilities. There were no taxes owed, and there were no unpaid water bills. Since it was on a septic field, we were able to get information about the age and condition of the septic system by calling the board of health. So we did some of our due diligence.

But we didn't do it all.

Matt showed up at the auction excited. Then he got to walk through the whole property—it was one of those very rare occasions when that's possible. He got to see the entire house. He calculated the ARV at around $320k and then backed out $30k for the estimated rehab cost to calculate his maximum bid. There was one other bidder, and the owner was there. She wasn't living in the property; she just attended the auction.

The bidding started, and it went back and forth between the other bidder and Matt. In the end Matt won it for $80k, his maximum bid. We were super happy. We handed over the $10k deposit and sent the paperwork to our lawyer.

And then our lawyer was like, "Did you realize this is a second lienholder? The second mortgage holder was foreclosing, not the first."

Wait, what?

Turns out there was a first mortgage of about $50k. We had quickly glanced at the registry of deeds during our due diligence and thought, "Oh, well this is the $80k one. And then there's a $50k one." We assumed that the $50k lien was the second lien, which would be wiped out as a result of the auction. But when determining lien priority, what's important is not the amount of the lien. What's important is when the lien was legally recorded. The "first lien" is the one that was legally recorded first. There's a saying people use to remember this rule, which is "First in time, first in kind."

In this case, the $80k lien was legally recorded a few hours after the $50k lien. Therefore, the first lien was $50k and the second lien was $80k—and the first lienholder wasn't the one foreclosing. The second lienholder was foreclosing, which meant that the $50k lien was still alive after the foreclosure auction. When a property is sold in a foreclosure auction, the winning bid satisfies the lien giving rise to the foreclosure and wipes out all lower-priority liens. Higher priority liens, however, aren't wiped out. They're still active on the property.

We had to choose between losing our $10k deposit or paying off the $50k first lien and moving on with the project. Luckily, there was still enough spread between the ARV and our winning bid price plus the rehab cost and the additional cost of paying off the first lien that we felt we would be okay financially. It wasn't as great a deal for us as it would have been without the additional $50k in cost, but it wasn't a total loser. We went through with buying the property, paid off the first lien, completed the rehab, and eventually sold the property and moved on—$50k lighter.

So, bummer move on our part.

GETTING A HEAD START WITH PREFORECLOSURES

On occasion we've been able to acquire distressed properties at a discount and avoid the competition of a foreclosure auction in what we call "preforeclosure." Here's how it works:

We learn that a foreclosure on a first mortgage is in process. Maybe the homeowner owes only $60k and the property is worth $200,000. We talk to the owner and offer to cure the lien by paying it off in exchange for the deed to the property. In addition, we also offer the homeowner money and time to move. In essence, we buy the property for the amount of the outstanding lien. The arrangement helps us because we don't compete with the bidders who might show up to the foreclosure auction. It helps the homeowner who both avoids having a foreclosure on their credit history and receives a little money and additional time to ease their transition to another housing arrangement. And it helps the lienholder because they recover the full amount of the lien. Since the house was headed to foreclosure already, it's a real win-win for everyone.

For the strategy to work, though, it's important to understand lien priority and thoroughly research whether other liens exist. That's because when a property is sold at a foreclosure auction, the sale wipes out all lower-priority liens behind the lien giving rise to the foreclosure. But since this purchase happens before a foreclosure ever takes place, all other outstanding liens on the property still survive after the deal closes.

One possible way to satisfy any other liens is to negotiate with the lienholders before finalizing the deal with the homeowner. We've negotiated with holders of mechanic's liens by telling them, for example, "You have a $5k lien. We'll buy it for $500. This house is already in foreclosure. If there's a foreclosure auction, you're going to get wiped out anyway and recover nothing on your lien."

We've successfully negotiated like this several times, and we've done it with banks as well. Kevin recently negotiated a deal on a two-family house in Westfield, Mass, that was in foreclosure as a result of a tax lien. When we told the local bank that their lien would get wiped out in the pending tax-lien foreclosure and offered a few thousand dollars for their $20k first-mortgage lien, they took it. Since we then owned the first mortgage, once we cured the tax lien we acquired the deed to the property free and clear.

For more info on buying property in preforeclosure, visit our YouTube channel, "Two Guys Take on Real Estate."

TYPES OF FORECLOSURE AUCTIONS

In addition to knowing the relevant state and local laws, it's also important to know the specific type of foreclosure happening to a property. The type of foreclosure—whether a bank foreclosure, tax foreclosure, HOA/COA foreclosure, or other rarer foreclosure—impacts how the process unfolds.

MORTGAGE FORECLOSURES

A mortgage foreclosure happens when a bank or other lender that lent money to the property owner to enable them to acquire the property forecloses on the property that secured the loan. When a property owner takes out a mortgage to buy a property, the lender places a lien on the property at that time. If the property owner later doesn't pay the mortgage, the lender can foreclose to recover the property owner's debt.

Most properties do not actually get sold to bidders at mortgage foreclosure auctions. In our experience, something like 85% go back to the lender after the foreclosure auction and become REOs. The property owners owe—and the lenders want to recoup—way more than most bidders are willing to pay at an auction. Banks often add massive lawyer fees to the liens in addition to the unpaid balance on the original mortgage note. Maybe the bank has paid the property taxes for five years while they waited to foreclose, and then they added interest on top of the taxes. The mortgage note might be $200k, but the bank takes the property back for $300k once they add the fees and taxes and interest.

We once went to an auction where we were the only bidder, so we thought we had a pretty good chance of winning. The mortgage note was $200k from 2014. We were only willing to bid $150k. The bank took the property back for almost $300k, because they were maintaining the lawn, paying taxes, then adding fines and fees to the lien.

TAX LIEN FORECLOSURES

Tax lien foreclosures are the result of nonpayment of property taxes to a local government, and they can be a fantastic way to get property cheap. A major reason is that in many states tax liens are known as "super-priority" liens, which means they are superior to all other liens on a property. In states where tax liens are super-priority liens, once the tax lien is cured in a foreclosure auction, all other liens on the property—first mortgages, second mortgages, COA or HOA liens, etc.—are wiped out. That makes them very attractive to acquire through foreclosure auction. It's also the reason why many, but not all, banks require that borrowers escrow property taxes when they take out a mortgage loan. This way, the bank protects its loan by taking over responsibility for paying the property taxes. The bank knows that if a borrower doesn't pay the property taxes, its lien will get wiped when the local government forecloses—so it wants to make sure the property taxes get paid.

The process for tax lien foreclosures varies from state to state and locality to locality. Some cities let property tax debts build up for years before they foreclose, while others will sit on properties for years after taking them back from the homeowners without hosting a foreclosure auction. By contrast, our hometown of Springfield hosts tax auctions every six months. They clean their books pretty quickly. Because they can make a windfall profit from the sale of foreclosed property, some cities will foreclose on properties for just a few thousand dollars in back taxes. We've seen people lose properties for pennies on the dollar relative to the value of the property tax debt. And unlike with bank foreclosure auctions, once a municipality hosts a foreclosure auction, all the proceeds from the sale belong to the municipality. The property owner gets nothing.

There are two dominant types of states with regard to tax liens: "tax lien certificate states" and "tax deed states." Some states do a hybrid of the two, and there are also "tax deed redeemable states." But tax lien certificate states and tax deed states are the two most common. Again, the key is to know the specific laws in the state where the property is located.

In tax lien certificate states, a local government issues a tax lien certificate when it tries to recover the property tax owed by a property owner. The local government will auction the lien for at least the amount that's owed in back taxes. The bidder who wins the auction is essentially buying the lien by paying off the back taxes, not the actual deed to the property. The buyer then gets the right to receive interest payments for a certain amount of time called the "redemption period" and subsequently to foreclose on the property once the redemption period ends if the property owner still hasn't paid the taxes. While the interest rates vary and can sometimes be negotiated as part of the bid, they're often 16% or more based on the value of the lien. For this reason, the interest alone can generate a nice income stream for investors.

During the redemption period, which is often six months or more, the property owner has time to "redeem" or pay off the tax liability. Meanwhile, the winning bidder receives interest payments based on the value of the lien. If the property owner pays off the back-owed tax, then the winning bidder receives the amount they paid for the back-owed tax plus the interest. If the property owner doesn't pay the back taxes during the redemption period, then the winning bidder has the right to foreclose and wipe out all lower-priority liens and acquire the property free and clear. At that point, the winning bidder works with a local attorney to file the proper foreclosure paperwork to enforce the lien and legally acquire the property. When the winning bidder completes the foreclosure, all other liens are wiped out because tax liens are super-priority liens.

In tax lien certificate states, buying tax liens can be a great way to get a nice return on your money, depending on the interest rate. If your real goal is to acquire property, though, then you have to be prepared that your money will be tied up for a while. Once you've won the property at a tax lien auction, you generally have another six to twelve months of possible redemption by the property owner. During that time you don't want to do any work on the property because if you do and the property owner pays the back taxes, you've just enriched their property at your expense. You're not entitled to get any of that money back. Still, it can be a great way to acquire a fantastic property very, very cheap if you can afford to wait the six- to twelve-month redemption period. Some tax liens are just a couple hundred dollars.

These auctions are typically—but not always—held online on the website for the local government that's pursuing the tax lien. Sometimes they're on the steps of the housing court. Regardless, information about them is usually available on the tax assessor's website.

Compared with tax lien certificate states, there's one big distinction in tax deed states: When you're buying a property at auction in most tax deed states, you're usually *buying the deed* rather than *buying the lien*. So foreclosures in tax deed states are more like bank foreclosures. Most of the time you don't have to wait through a redemption period before you own the property. In contrast to the process in tax lien certificate states, no interest payments are involved since there's no redemption period. The property has already gone through the tax collection process, so the city or county is foreclosing rather than selling its tax lien. Because tax liens are super-priority liens, then all lower-priority liens on the property—first mortgages, second mortgages, and the like—have been wiped out by the time the winning bidder acquires the property by foreclosure auction.

Auctions in tax deed states can also be held online or at the city or county hall. You can go on the tax assessor's website for information about how they handle their tax lien foreclosures. And you can often get properties cheap, especially if not a lot of people show up to the auction.

As always, be mindful of the laws of the state where the property is located when buying properties as a result of tax-lien foreclosures, because some states with tax deeds still have a redemption period. Whether you're in a tax lien certificate state or a tax deed state with a redemption period, you don't want to put too much money or work into the property until the redemption period. There is the potential that the property owner could come back, pay the back taxes, and reclaim the property. Some states have a one-year redemption period, others like Connecticut have a two-year redemption period. Each state is a little different.

We once had five tax deeds that we won at auction in Connecticut that we had to sit on for two years before we could sell them. We had over $100k tied up for over two years. If you can't sit on that kind of money for that long, it can be a real burden. Before investing in tax liens, know your state laws so that you don't get caught holding the bag when you really want to keep the velocity of your money moving.

One more thing to keep in mind: Tax liens are some of the most common unforeseen liabilities that come up with foreclosed property. If you don't know how to research them, who to call for information, or how to look at the registry deeds, you should hire a lawyer to perform a title rundown for you so that you can have a better idea of whether there's also $20k in outstanding tax liens on the property you plan to buy at a bank foreclosure auction.

HOA/COA FORECLOSURES

State laws dictate the treatment of condominium owners' association and homeowners' association liens for unpaid fees. In some states, like Massachusetts, they're considered super-liens that supersede bank liens but are subordinate to tax liens. In states that consider COA and HOA liens to be super-liens, bank liens get wiped out in the event that a condo association forecloses. In other states, like Connecticut, a COA foreclosure doesn't wipe out any mortgage liens. You will still have to consider whether there are any bank or municipal tax liens on the property, but if your court system is online, then you can search for the court documents for that type of lien. Once you've done the due diligence on the laws in your state and on whether any other liens exist, you could still have a higher probability of success of acquiring the property cheaply as a result of an association lien.

Where we live, there are third-party auctioneers who specialize in condo foreclosures. In Massachusetts, homeowners' associations also have to file a form with the courts before they can foreclose. In states that require a similar process, typically you can find a list of foreclosures or a list of the auctioneers on the state's website.

In states where COA and HOA liens are super-liens, these foreclosures can be a fantastic way to buy property really cheap. We've bought properties worth a couple hundred grand for just $1k.

A NEAR MISS

We were wrapping up our due diligence on a condo foreclosure we'd found in Connecticut. We assumed that it would be handled like every other condo foreclosure we'd been to in Massachusetts, where condo liens are super-priority liens that wipe out any bank lienholders. Matt headed out to the auction, ready to bid.

Then one of our other partners piped in right before the auction: "Hold on. Let's look into this opportunity a little deeper, in case something is different. I just have a gut feeling…"

So Matt scrambled to read up on the law right before the auction. Turns out, condo associations in Connecticut can only recover the first nine months of condo fees, and a foreclosure auction does not wipe out bank liens. In other words, association liens are not super-priority liens in Connecticut. Therefore a winning bidder would still be responsible for the mortgage balance.

This condo was worth about $175k ARV. We knew that the minimum bid would be $11k, leaving a potential spread of $164k. Before taking into account any mortgage lien, we were like "Wow, we'll bid here!" We knew that the outstanding mortgage balance was $120k, but we thought the bank would get wiped out, so who cared?

Turns out, the bank debt didn't get wiped out. If we'd gone ahead with our bid and won the auction for $11k based on our knowledge of the law in Massachusetts without double-checking the law in Connecticut, we would have been liable for paying off the bank's $120k. Which would have made it a very sad day for us.

OTHER FORECLOSURES

While bank, tax, and association liens are the most common that lead to foreclosure auctions, you may occasionally run across other less common liens in foreclosure. For instance, in Massachusetts we run across receivership liens that result from a municipality taking over an abandoned or neglected property. If the owner of a property is unwilling or unable to keep the house up to code, eventually the city will bring suit before a judge to have a contractor assigned to the property to do the work. Whatever expense the contractor racks up to bring the property into compliance becomes a super-priority lien on the property. If the owner can't or won't pay, the contractor can foreclose on the lien.

The cool thing is that lien supersedes all the other liens on the property. So if the property has ten mortgages on it and bad debts that resulted in liens on the property, those liens are all blown out by this one lien. And if nobody else shows up at the auction to bid on the house, the contractor could buy the house for just the cost of his own lien—which probably included some decent markup. The contractor is not doing the work for free, so he essentially acquires the house for his cost.

Most states have some type of receivership law in place, but they all handle it differently. Even in Mass, each municipality handles them differently—Springfield will vary from Worcester—and they keep changing.

In a receivership lien situation, there are two opportunities for investors. The first is bidding on the job as contractor under the receivership. The second is bidding at the auction if and when the contractor forecloses on the lien for payment.

BIDDING ON THE JOB AS CONTRACTOR UNDER THE RECEIVERSHIP

We've actually acquired properties this way. We've done over fifty receiverships as the contractors and acquired more than eighty units. We once had a 200-unit complex under receivership. But new judges have made it stricter and stricter. The process is very paper-intensive, and it's gotten even worse. Before we got into it, receiverships were like the Wild West where contractors could charge whatever they wanted for the work they did. Contractors were getting away with murder. We stepped in and even advised on some of the changes to the process, but now the changes have gone way too far—to the point where fewer and fewer people do receiverships because it's just not profitable anymore. Contractors can't work for free, and the process ties up your money for years as you try to go through the court process to get paid.

As a result, receiverships attract mostly contractors and professional investors. You have to be approved by the court to do the rehab work, and then you're working as an arm of the court. The court performs a background check to make sure you have the right licensing and that you have the funds to handle the job.

BIDDING ON THE RECEIVERSHIP LIEN FORECLOSURE AUCTION

The foreclosure auction that often results from a receivership lien is a public auction anybody can attend. Whether it produces a good deal or not depends on whether the contractor who did the work intends to bid. If the contractor who did the work intends to buy the property at auction, they will most likely win because they've got a huge advantage over any other bidders. Often they will bid the full lien amount knowing the lien includes their profit markup, and then close out their own lien for less than the full amount.

That said, some contractors take receiverships only as a way to get work and never intend to buy the property. It can be an attractive source of income because receivership contract work is at the prevailing wage, full price. The contractors don't have to deal with Sally Homeowner saying, "Can't you do a little bit better on the price? I don't really like my bathroom job." Contractors can just tell the judge, "We charge $75 an hour for this. We charge $120 bucks an hour for that. We did twenty hours. Here's the total cost." The judge reviews the invoices and most of the time says, "That sounds about right." When the foreclosure auction happens, the contractor is happy to watch somebody bid and win because that means they're going to get paid in full. And they're making very healthy margins as opposed to working for individual homeowners who would be a pain in the butt.

In this situation, a receivership lien foreclosure auction could be a great opportunity for an owner-occupier to buy a fully renovated property at less than market value. If you were to go this route, you'd have another advantage in that there's a whole report on the condition of the property and all the work that was done by the receiver. You can find out if there's an upgraded kitchen, for instance.

GO PRO

Before you dive into buying properties in foreclosure auctions, we recommend that you develop a network of professionals who can advise you along the way. Whether you're buying property at a foreclosure auction or even just managing property rentals in general, you can't know everything. It's also easier to scale when you hire professionals and put a team and systems in place that allow you to grow more safely and reliably versus just doing it all on your own. Trying to be a jack-of-all-trades and a master of none generally doesn't work. We tried. Remember our very first house? We'd rather have a bunch of masters around us.

For most people buying foreclosure property, it's a good idea to work with an attorney—and not just a general practice attorney, but an attorney who specializes in real estate. In general, every state is going to have its own special nuances to the foreclosure process. Every state is going to have different landlord-tenant laws. Every property will be subject to state and local zoning laws as well as laws on health and safety, which deal with issues ranging from lead paint and asbestos to septic systems and building codes.

Because we run real estate businesses with lots of moving parts, we actually have four different lawyers on retainer. One handles our commercial property, another handles our corporation, and a third specializes in employment law. Then there's the one who handles all our landlord-tenant cases. She also handles Kev, for which she's earned a special place in heaven.

A CAUTIONARY TALE

So here's a good example of what not to do, because we made such a minor mistake but got hammered for it.

We bought an older, owner-occupied home at a foreclosure auction. After we closed, we reached out to work with the occupants on getting them out. We made contact with the wife; the husband was getting out of jail around that time. We reached an agreement that they would pay $1k per month for use-in-occupancy in exchange for two additional months of time to vacate. The amount was a good bit less than market rent, but at least it covered some of our holding costs. It also bought the former owners time to make a plan to move on. We thought it was a good deal all around. So they signed an agreement to that effect. They even signed a statement saying the house was safe and habitable.

After we made that agreement, we then wholesaled the property to an investor whom we told, "Don't worry about the occupants. They agreed to leave, and we have a signed contract with them. We're cool." So we closed the deal with the wholesale buyer and thought we'd scored another win.

In the meantime, we needed to stop by the house again to check on something. This time when we reached out to the occupants, they stopped being cooperative. Instead, they said, "Hey, listen. We talked to an attorney, and you had no right to have us sign the agreement we signed. It's not legally binding. We're not paying you the money we told you we would pay. You stay away from our property! That's an illegal, nonbinding agreement. We're not paying you anything. We're not going anywhere." And we were like, "What the hell?!"

We went by a week later and knocked on the back door. The former owners didn't answer. We walked around the house and knocked on the side door from the driveway. No answer. We then walked around to the front of the house and saw somebody peeking out from behind the curtain. We motioned to them like, "Hi. Going over there to knock on your door." But they wouldn't open that door either. They were clearly ignoring us.

They'd already told us they weren't going to pay the rent. We had a contract that said, "You can stay for two months in exchange for $1k for use and occupancy due on the 15th." It wasn't yet the 15th at that point, but they had already told us they weren't going to honor the contract. Why not just start an eviction because they were clearly not going to pay? By that time we'd already given them three additional weeks in the house. So, we sent them a notice to vacate. Why wait any longer? Eviction is a long process.

The problem was: We sent that notice before the payment was due, so technically they had not yet defaulted on the agreement. Their payment was due on the 15th, and we sent them a notice to vacate on the 13th. Essentially we terminated the agreement with them before they had violated it, even though they told us they were not going to live up to it. That was our first mistake.

The occupants went to those ridiculous ambulance-chasing lawyers who really dig in and find every possible argument. They claimed that we had intentionally tried to deceive the occupants by writing up our agreement on the wrong form. We had used for the agreement a form provided by the housing court in Massachusetts. It's a form you use when you go to court for an eviction case, and you want to work out a deal in the hallway right before your case gets heard. Instead of going in front of the judge, the parties can use this agreement template to settle their differences and avoid court. We've probably used it hundreds if not thousands of times to settle eviction cases with our tenants.

The problem with that was: The form mentions something along the lines of "instead of having a case in front of a judge, the parties hereby agree…." We used the form thinking it was a logical form to use when you're making an agreement with somebody to avoid an eviction. But the bottom line was, we were not in court when we made the agreement. We didn't even have a court case when we made the agreement. It was an honest mistake—but a costly one.

Basically the attorneys were like, "Listen, you were using unfair and deceptive business practices with unsophisticated people, leading them to believe you had a case against them. You lied to them. You deceived them into thinking they were in court. This document is a court agreement. But you had no court case. There was no court case!" So we got nailed on that.

And then the lawyers claimed, "You guys made an agreement and then you terminated it and tried to evict them before they could have even lived up to the agreement. That's crazy! What were you thinking? And then you're walking around the property at all times of day and night peeping into the windows…" We weren't peeping in the windows, we were trying to talk to the tenants! They were peeping out from the windows!

The lawyers countersued us and our wholesale buyer, and accused us of being really bad actors. In addition to paying all the legal fees for the wholesale buyer—who never did business with us again—we ended up settling the case for the $80k. On top of that, the former owners got to keep the house. So they got the house and $80k because of really minor transgressions on our part: filing for eviction too early and using the wrong form of agreement. It's not like we were on the property with ski masks and baseball bats doing underhanded stuff. We went out to the property and had a conversation, "Hey, you live here. We own the house now. We want you to leave. Can you be out by the weekend? Oh, you need some time? Okay. We want to sell the house tomorrow, but I guess we could let you buy some time. If you need two months, how about you pay us while you figure out your plan?" That's what we did—or tried to do. We just didn't run it by our attorney first.

That's why we don't wholesale occupied properties anymore.

Especially if you're considering buying an occupied property, make sure you have a skilled housing attorney with expertise in landlord-tenant laws advising you every step of the way. Throughout this book we talk in general terms about both how the foreclosure process works and what we have to do to comply with landlord-tenant laws in Massachusetts and Connecticut where we operate, but you should know your state laws and do your own due diligence because we can't give everyone all the information for every state. We can say in general, "This has been our experience in Massachusetts" or "This has been our experience in Connecticut." But unless you live where we live, your state and municipality will almost undoubtedly be different from ours.

So who are the other masters who should be in your network? First, let's start with who you probably don't need in it. Unlike when you're buying a nonforeclosure property, you don't necessarily need a home inspector. You might really want a home inspector, but realistically a home inspector is not going to help you. The home inspector is probably not going to get access inside the house before the auction and before you place your bid. Even if the home inspector gets access to the house and gives you a report after you win the auction, it won't help you. Because the sale in a foreclosure auction is "as is, where is," you can't renegotiate the purchase price after the auction is over.

That said, you likely will benefit from having a knowledgeable contractor on your team who can go with you to the auction, or even take a look at the property prior to the auction and give you realistic bids for the work that will need to be done if you win. Either you need to know how to estimate all the costs involved in your investment or you need a really good contractor who can give you that info. That's the key: If you don't have that knowledge, then you need to find someone who does and make them part of your team. They don't necessarily need to be a business partner. You could let them know you plan to flip five houses a year and you want them to be your go-to contractor. Make sure they have the knowledge that they speak. Trust but verify.

To give you an example of why: Matt was at the auction of a little house that needed a lot of work. The ARV of the house was probably $225k, but it needed at least $50k of work to get it there. When the auction opened, there was only one other bidder. Matt could have won it for $92k. Based on just those numbers, there was a potential profit of $83k. But the property was an hour away, which would mean additional cost for either travel or local contractors. Matt also added the holding costs for ten weeks. Once he added up the total cost based on his years of experience, the profit margin became smaller and smaller. So he passed.

As soon as possible after you close on the property you've won, you'll want to get your contractors into it to draw up the scope of work so that they can start working. A general contractor (GC) might have specialists already on their team such as HVAC technicians, electricians, and plumbers. But if the GC doesn't have the specialists you need or if you're like us and prefer to have more direct control over the professionals working on your property, then it's a good idea to bring these folks onto your team in advance. Get all your contractors lined up early in the process so that you have maximum ability to coordinate their work and minimize the amount of time the rehab takes.

Ever since Our Worst Deal Ever (as discussed in Chapter 1), we make sure to request and then read our contractors' insurance policies to verify that they're insured for the work they're going to perform for us. They may tell you they can do the work, but doing the work and *being insured to do the work* are two different things. So talk to their insurance agent. Or better yet, have their insurance agent talk to your insurance agent, especially if you don't have the knowledge or patience to read and really understand an insurance policy. We can hand our insurance broker the policy for a contractor we're interested in hiring and ask, "Does this policy cover the contractor for XYZ?" Lastly, make sure you also get added as an "additional insured" on the contractor's policy so you are clearly covered for the work the contractor will perform and can rest easy that the contractor's insurance company will pay you out in the event of a claim. It's a very common business practice, it's easy to do, and yet people generally forget to request it.

Depending on your goal for the property, you may need additional people in your network. If your intention is to flip the property or to wholesale it, for instance, then well in advance of the auction you'll want to develop your list of potential buyers or investors who will scoop the property up from you. That way, you don't have to hold onto it very long. You could potentially flip the contract to your buyer without ever having to own the property. Some banks will allow an "assignable contract," which means the auction winner can assign the contract to another buyer. If your exit strategy for the property is to flip the contract to a wholesale buyer or investor, then it's a good idea to have a long list of potential buyers in your pocket.

We've also found it helpful to network with other foreclosure buyers. They might share inside information about the property, or they might lead you to great contractors or other professionals like attorneys who specialize in housing law. We don't like to be adversarial with other bidders at the auctions we attend for this reason: You catch more flies with honey than with vinegar. That strategy has worked well for us; being open and honest with the other bidders and not waging a battle against each other. We've found it helpful to be friendly and to develop a mutual respect. At times they've given us tips, and we've shared tips as well.

That said, there are a few things to keep in mind when you're dealing with other bidders. First, avoid collusion. For instance, at a foreclosure auction the bidders are not supposed to agree not to bid because it doesn't create fair bidding. We've attended auctions where one bidder offered another $5k not to bid. That kind of collusion does happen, but it's not technically legal. Also, be aware that not everyone at a foreclosure auction is necessarily trustworthy. And if they're not trustworthy, then they might try to mislead you. Their inside tip might be an exaggeration or even a lie designed to scare you from bidding.

If your intention is to rent out the property, or even if not but the property is occupied, then it's a really good idea to find yourself a skilled housing attorney.

FINDING THE AUCTIONS

Online searches are your best bet for finding foreclosure auctions. As you're searching, keep in mind that there's a difference between a "foreclosure" and a "foreclosure auction." You'll want to search specifically for "foreclosure auction." Often when websites mention "foreclosures," they're referring to properties that have already gotten foreclosed. They're REOs and not properties headed to a foreclosure *auction*. So, make sure to search for foreclosure auctions in your target area, and not just foreclosures. We don't use subscription foreclosure websites that claim to aggregate information because we're able to access what we need for free.

Because most states require that a foreclosure auction be announced in a public notice, there are likely a small handful of places—most of them free—where you can find information about upcoming auctions. In some states, and especially in judicial states, information about foreclosure auctions is accessible on a government website. Connecticut puts all the information about the foreclosure auction on a website including when it's happening, the docket number, a property appraisal, and other due diligence. If you're tech-savvy, you can go onto their court database and find all that information. You can do a lot of due diligence that the court has already done for you right there, which is awesome. But that also means that everyone else has the ability to see that information, so it's a double-edged sword.

Even in nonjudicial states where lienholders don't have to get a judge's approval to foreclose, they still have to follow certain steps. Typically those steps include posting a legal notice of foreclosure in a local newspaper. Not a lot of people use physical newspapers these days, but most newspapers also have an online database. We regularly look at our local newspapers' websites for public notices about upcoming foreclosure auctions.

In Massachusetts, lienholders typically use third-party auctioneers to conduct foreclosure auctions. Most, but not all, third-party auctioneers maintain websites. They're trying to drive as many people to the auction as possible, so they'll update the website with the when and where of the foreclosure auctions they're handling. We keep a list of all the third-party foreclosure auctioneers in our state and check their websites routinely. You're going to want to Google "foreclosure auctions" in your state and find all the different auctioneers. You might also be able to go to the state licensure website and look up the licensed auctioneers and find their names and then Google their company names to find their websites.

TWO GUYS TAKE ON WHAT YOU NEED TO KNOW BEFORE YOU GO

- There are a limited number and type of debts that can result in a lien that can lead to a foreclosure on a property.

- The entire process is often lengthy—years rather than months.

- The terms of foreclosure auctions are typically "as is, where is," which means you're buying the property literally as you see it.

- One major factor that impacts the foreclosure process and therefore impacts foreclosure buyers is whether the state where the property is located is a "judicial foreclosure state" or a "nonjudicial foreclosure state."

- Before you bid on a property in a foreclosure auction, it's important to understand "lien priority."

- The type of foreclosure—whether a mortgage foreclosure, tax foreclosure, association foreclosure or other rarer foreclosure—impacts how the process unfolds.

- Before you dive into buying properties in foreclosure auctions, we recommend you develop a network of professionals who can advise you along the way.

- Online searches using free websites, including government, local newspaper, and auctioneers, are your best bet for finding foreclosure auctions.

CHAPTER 3

TRAIN YOUR BRAIN

One word sums up the mindset a person should have before buying a property at a foreclosure auction: *cautious.*

There's so much that can go wrong. We have learned that fortune does not always favor the bold. Remember, you're buying a property at a foreclosure auction "as is, where is." That means that 99% of the time, you're not getting inside it before the auction begins. No matter how much you try to research beforehand, there's inherently so much you can't know. And if the property is occupied, you're going to have headaches. A lot of them.

The best way to prepare for your first foreclosure auction is to get into the right mindset and learn as much as you can. You have to go into the process believing that you can succeed. It's almost like people have been brainwashed, especially in recent years, that they "can't." They jokingly call it "The Oppression Olympics." Everyone wants to tell you why they can't succeed; why they're being held down by this, that, and the other thing; and why they're in a category of people who just don't have a fair shot at anything. It's crazy, but it's really easy to buy into that belief because it's harder to succeed than to fail. It's really easy to fail. So it's a matter of shaking off that perception of reality that "everybody is struggling" and realize that, in fact, many people are succeeding. And for everybody who doesn't try, it makes it that much easier for somebody else who does.

Then be willing to put in the time and effort. Besides reading this book and following us on YouTube, attend some auctions with the intention to just watch and learn the process. Talk to other bidders, talk to the auctioneers. They have a wealth of knowledge and will probably happily share their experience. Usually people aren't that secretive in this business.

In our experience, being bold and ballsy when performing due diligence helps a lot when it comes to buying property in foreclosure. We've been chased off properties by occupants threatening to shoot. It doesn't happen often, maybe once a year. As part of our due diligence, we try to get the occupant's permission to walk around a property to evaluate it. Sometimes the occupants—often the owners—threaten us with bodily harm.

It's important to have the balls and the confidence to knock on the door of someone who's getting foreclosed on in an hour and try to talk to them about the property. If we don't, we could miss something big like a foundation issue. You need to be able to talk to town officials about the property you might buy, and talk to potential neighbors to get the inside scoop on the property or the occupants.

MY, WHAT BIG EYES YOU HAVE

We won a single-family house in southern Mass that had been abandoned for a long time. When we got the deed forty days later, Matt drove down to the property as per our usual process to secure it.

When he got there, he went right to work. First, he drilled out the old locks on all the doors and popped in new ones. Then he started the rundown of his inspection checklist as he performed a thorough walk-through. He made sure all the windows were secure and locked. He confirmed the sources of all the utilities (municipal water or well; septic field or sewer line; oil, gas, or electric heat, etc.), and made sure there was plenty of fuel by inspecting and photographing all the meters. He wrote down the meter numbers so he'd have them when he called the electric and gas companies to get the services turned on. He took pictures of everything as he went along, just in case we needed them later.

As he walked around, Matt noticed a lot of little pieces of garbage everywhere. The amount was unusual, but you never know with these vacant properties, so he didn't think much of it. At last, he made his way toward a little loft area above the garage. He started climbing a set of ladder-like steps, and as he approached the top, he was met by several sets of eyes.

Matt stopped, totally freaked out. Then the biggest of the raccoons came at him. Matt stumbled back down the ladder and booked it out of the loft area.

The raccoons didn't seem amenable to negotiating an exit, so we had to evict them. We contacted our local pest control guy who takes care of all our properties. He set a series of traps to catch them for "rehoming" somewhere else. It ended up being a whole family of seven or eight raccoons: a mother, a father, and a bunch of babies. Kev is still bummed he didn't get to adopt one.

They'd apparently been nesting in the insulation for quite some time. We had to rip it all out and start over. Not exactly a box of chocolates, but you still never know what you're gonna get.

A sense of humor helps too. Number one: crazy things happen when you're buying foreclosures. You might meet someone chomping on a stick of butter. You just have to laugh. Number two: it's helped us build really great relationships with the auctioneers and other professional bidders in our area who don't treat us like the competition. It makes sense to develop good relationships with these folks because you will see a lot of them if you attend foreclosure auctions regularly.

We also think you need to have a solid understanding of how to run the numbers to analyze a potential deal and the fortitude to stick to them. That's just good business sense. We got in trouble once when we worked with a partner who was not so diligent about that. He'd try to dollar-cost-average the properties we bought: "We're making a profit on the property we won this morning, so we can take a little loss on the property we're bidding on this afternoon." We would tell him "No, that strategy doesn't make sense because we haven't made any money yet. We haven't even closed on the first one. Stick to the numbers." But he wouldn't always listen. Then after we actually got inside the house or thoroughly inspected the property, we'd find out that we didn't do as well as we initially thought on that first one. And because we went so aggressive on the second one, profit margins that once looked healthy started getting thin. In fact, we'd overextended our finances. So then we were stuck. We had to work twice as hard to make no money on two deals because we weren't as cautious and conservative as we should have been. Now we run our numbers, figure out our maximum bid, and really don't go above it. If it's $41k, then it's $41k, not $41,500.

It's also important to have a clear goal for the property you plan to buy. If you have a very definitive goal, you can tailor how you want to go about auctions and your bidding strategy. If you're buying and holding, or if you're flipping, or if you're buying your home, that's going to change what you want to bid on and how you'll bid. For example, if you know your goal is to acquire ten rental properties in your neighborhood or city, then you can hone down your list of possible properties. You can learn all about the foreclosures in that area and get to know all the auctioneers. Then you can just focus on the properties that match your goal as opposed to not knowing and not having a focus. If you're looking at all these different auctions when they don't really meet your criteria, you're wasting a lot of your time. Be hyper-focused. Then you can spend your time on the due diligence for properties that will work for you. Especially if you're a homeowner, you need to know exactly what you want. Don't waste your time going to a hundred auctions for properties you know don't meet your criteria.

Once you have a clear idea of your goal, you'll also need a little patience. Depending on how many properties you plan to buy, you may have to attend dozens or even hundreds of auctions. On average we attend twenty auctions a week. Maybe 15% of the properties at bank foreclosure auctions we see end up in the hands of a third party. Often the banks take them back for a lot more than any bidder is willing to pay, and then the properties become REOs. If you go to one hundred auctions, only ten to fifteen of the properties will actually go to a bidder.

The ability to adapt is critical when buying these properties. Once you do win an auction, not everything will go according to plan. In fact, often things won't go according to plan. As Robert Jordan (one of Kev's favorite authors) wrote, "The best plan lasts until the first arrow leaves the bow." Or to put it the way Mike Tyson did before his fight with Evander Holyfield, "Everybody has a plan until they get punched in the mouth." And that's just the way it is when you're buying properties at foreclosure auctions.

It's going to help you survive if you learn to adapt to whatever comes up and whatever obstacle ends up standing in your way. Sometimes just like water, you can't go through a barrier. You have to change course and go around it. So have an intention or plan or goal, but then don't be rigid about it. If you're rigid when buying foreclosures, you'll only damage yourself, slow yourself down, or hurt yourself in the process. Instead, be like water and take the path of least resistance to your destination.

When you find yourself in that situation with a tenant or a rehab that's going awry, you can't wake up every day and ask, "What the hell? I can't believe it's taking so long! It's been three months!" When you're in the process and doing everything you can to move it along, the rest is out of your hands. Getting through the process means accepting that it's going to take some time in some cases, and there's nothing you can do about that. No sense in beating yourself up about it or being all stressed. If you're in for a three-month ordeal, you're in for a three-month ordeal.

Often that takes determination as well. For example, when we found out there was a couple living in the barn of a house we'd just bought, we were determined to figure out a way to get what we wanted and needed—which was to have a vacant property, to do our project, and to not lose our shirts in the process—while also not making a homeless, elderly veteran who served our country live under a bridge. It was very challenging because he was shutting us down and ignoring us. Just simply communicating with him took an incredible amount of patience because he was hard of hearing, and logistically we could only communicate in person, no phone, email, or Zoom. But everybody involved was trying to do the right thing. Everybody really just kept their head down and said, "No, we're going to figure this out. We're going to figure this out." And we were determined to do it in such a way that we could still be successful and make something out of the property. So when challenges come up, you need to be really determined to find a good, ethical way to operate while keeping in mind that you also have to be profitable.

Profitability and good business sense drive empathy. You don't need to be told to do the right thing when the right thing ends up being what makes you money. Put it this way: If we win a property that's occupied, we don't want to avoid evicting the occupant because we're empathetic, because we're good guys who hate to see someone lose their home. We *are* good guys (well, at least one of us is), and we *don't like* all these bad things to happen to people. We don't want to evict somebody, because it makes business sense to solve the issue that's causing the need to evict them instead. It's a happy coincidence that empathy lines up with good business sense.

If we're working with a tenant who's not paying us in our rental business, we want to help them find employment, create a payment plan, be stable, and get the tenancy back on track because it costs us a ton of money to evict somebody. Once we evict them, we have to renovate and market the vacant apartment. All the months it's vacant, we're losing 100% of its income. So just from a business standpoint, we don't want to evict somebody because it costs so much money. We want to avoid it.

Now, from an empathetic standpoint, it's the exact same thing. We don't want to evict somebody because it creates hardship for them. It also makes us sad. We want to find a way to avoid that. So, the two things end up correlating. If you wish to operate a business solely on empathy, the good thing is your empathetic practices will probably keep you in business because you're making smart choices. If you want to operate your business solely based on business practices and empathy doesn't factor in, then you're going to try to find the right way to keep your costs down, which usually means helping keep people in their homes. In our experience, empathy comes with good business decisions and vice versa. It really does line up.

TWO GUYS TAKE ON TRAINING YOUR BRAIN

- One word sums up the mindset a person should have before buying a property at a foreclosure auction: cautious.

- The best way to prepare for your first foreclosure auction is to get into the right mindset and learn as much as you can. That means:

    - Being bold and ballsy about your due diligence Having a sense of humor

    - Understanding how to run the numbers— and having the fortitude to stick to them

    - Having clear goals for the property you plan to buy

    - Being a little patient

    - Adapting when a challenge arises

    - Exercising good business sense

SECTION II

CHOOSE YOUR OWN FORECLOSURE

We want our real estate book on investing to be novel. Not a novel. But not boring like most of the other books on real estate investing that Kev has never read. Matt has read them, though, and he thinks they don't really prepare you for what you'll find at foreclosure auctions. Because you're going to find—well, God only knows what you're going to find.

And that's the point. You will almost certainly find the unexpected, and we want you to experience what it's like for yourself. That's why this next section of the book is in the style of a popular children's book series called Choose Your Own Adventure, which Kev did read, and not even that long ago.

Here's your chance to choose your own foreclosure. How are you going to fund it? What did you find in your due diligence? And what are you going to do with that former homeowner still living in your property?

Choose wisely and maybe you'll end up with a vacant property. Choose unwisely and who knows? Maybe you'll end up being the one in foreclosure.

Good luck!

CHAPTER 4

MONEY, MONEY, MONEY

Making your plan to access capital should be one of the first things you do. Educating yourself on the foreclosure process comes first, but the very next step to work on is getting funding. Then make sure you have the funds ready for both the initial purchase *and* the subsequent rehab before you attend your first foreclosure auction as a bidder.

Unless you're going to an auction for informational purposes only (which we highly recommend, by the way), there's no point in attending as an active participant until you have the financial wherewithal to purchase the property. If you place a bid at a foreclosure auction and your bid wins the auction, then you are legally obligated to close the deal or lose your deposit. It would be risky to win an auction and *then* try to hustle and find the money to close the deal and complete whatever work you intend to do next. We're not saying it's impossible, but it would not be the smartest approach. However you go about finding liquid cash or access to capital, do it ahead of time. Get a plan in place before you go to the auction.

And remember: You're not just coming up with the money to buy the house; you're coming up with the money to *renovate* the house as well. If the house is going to cost $150k to buy, you still need to have the money to carry it and renovate it. So when you're borrowing that hard money for the initial purchase, you're also borrowing rehab money and holding cost money.

We'll talk about calculating your maximum allowable bid a little later, but when you're at an auction looking at a property, you're calculating the total cost of the project to figure out what you're willing to bid. You need to acquire the capital to cover *all* those costs. Otherwise, you'll have the money to buy the house but then realize, "Crap. I don't have the money for all the materials, the labor, the taxes, and the water bill," whatever it might be to hold it. "Shoot. I forgot about that part." You can't go back and ask for more money, so you want to arrange the funding for all that at once.

We'll go over several options for accessing capital that we're familiar with, some of which we've used ourselves at one time or another. Keep in mind, though, that this is not an exhaustive list of all the possible ways you can fund your purchase. This is just a high level of options to get your wheels turning. We recommend that if you're starting down the path of real estate investing, do your research and talk to a financial advisor.

FUNDING THE DEPOSIT

If you're like a lot of people we talk to who believe they can't get into the foreclosure game, one of the biggest barriers is the deposit. There's a common belief that you need to come to the auction with cash—a lot of cash. But that's not always the case. The amount of money required on the day of the foreclosure auction actually varies widely from state to state, and can range from as little as a few thousand dollars to the full purchase price. And, just to be clear, most auctioneers want a check these days, not cash. They used to allow cash, but most now want a certified bank check for the deposit.

In Massachusetts where we've attended hundreds if not thousands of foreclosure auctions, most require a $5k or $10k deposit. That makes it really easy for almost anyone to come in and bid. But it's also true that in some states, especially judicial states, you must bid at the auction with a substantial sum in hand for the deposit. In Texas, for example, you must go to the foreclosure auction with a check for the whole purchase amount; whatever you're willing to bid, even if it's $200k or $300k, you need a check for that amount. But we don't mess with Texas.

While having a big deposit like that is a challenge for a lot of folks, it's also an opportunity. If you can work out the funding in advance, you have a huge advantage because fewer people are going to come to the auction. Think about it: Most people can get access to $5k. We love auctions in Connecticut, a judicial state where there's a high deposit amount, because that generally means less competition for us. In Connecticut we often skip auctions where the deposits are under $20k because that's where we see a horde of people. But when the deposit requirement gets over $50k, most people don't want to tie up that much money while they wait to close on the property. So if you can figure out the solution to ensure you have the money and access funds, there will be less people and less competition then.

Funding the purchase really comes down to two broad options: tapping your own resources or leveraging other people's money. If you're creative, you may have more access to capital than you think.

CHOOSE YOUR OWN ADVENTURE

If you want to get creative about
tapping your own resources, *keep reading.*

If you want to explore ***leveraging other people's money***, *turn to page 95.*

If you want to read about the ***options if your credit score isn't great***, *turn to page 119.*

TAPPING YOUR OWN RESOURCES

Some people do have $50k or $75k in savings or a 401(k) or another retirement account that they could borrow against to fund the purchase of a property. If that's you, well done! Now put that money to good use to kick off your real estate investment strategy.

RAID THAT RETIREMENT ACCOUNT

First, talk to a CPA who deals specifically with real estate investing about all your options. Even if there are penalties for accessing your funds, the deal could be worth it. It just depends on your risk-reward appetite and how much the penalties cost you. If you'll be hit with a 10% penalty but the deal provides a solid 20% return, dude, why wouldn't you? But not everyone has that appetite.

Then talk to the custodians or administrators of all your retirement accounts about options for using the funds you've already saved. If you have a 401(k) at work with a balance, talk to your 401k representative about leveraging that money. The representative will know how the plan is structured, and if it allows loans against it. Every plan is a little different. There's not just one tried and true method to establish the rules of a 401(k). The plan administrator will know the details of what the plan allows and what percentage of the assets can be borrowed. Some plans allow a 50% Loan-to-Value (LTV) ratio, for instance, so if you have $100k saved, you can only borrow $50k.

If you already have an Individual Retirement Account (IRA) that's not self-directed, you may be able to transfer it into a self-directed IRA (SDIRA) and then use the assets in it to fund your real estate investments. The investments themselves would then be held in the SDIRA.

What makes an IRA "self-directed" is the fact that you as the account holder get to manage the investments in it. While a custodian still administers the account, you have much more discretion over your investment selections. Best of all, an SDIRA can include alternative investments that aren't typically allowed in a "regular" IRA. SDIRAs can be either traditional or Roth IRAs.

The key is finding a custodian who knows how to handle SDIRAs, especially if you're going to use one to buy real estate. It's not a product you can just set up with Fidelity or Vanguard. You need to find someone who knows what they're doing because there are a lot of stops involved in setting it up properly. If you miss any of the steps, you could violate the law and IRS codes—and then the IRS will say the transaction is null and void for tax purposes and tax you on it. So, find a good professional who is already an experienced custodian for SDIRAs.

One of our partners uses his SDIRA to fund real estate transactions, and it's worked well for him and our business. It can definitely be a great use of retirement funds.

LEVERAGE YOUR HOME EQUITY

If you don't have any personal funds by way of savings or retirement accounts but you already own a home, you might be able to tap your home's equity. You may have access to more money than you think by way of your own personal house that you've been living in for ten years. You've paid the mortgage down. Maybe like so many people, you've seen massive appreciation on your house in the last few years. Your house jumped in value, and all of a sudden, wow, you have major equity! You're only at 50% LTV. Tap that equity.

Many people are familiar with home equity loans (also known as second mortgages) and home equity lines of credit (HELOC). Contact your mortgage company or bank that can advise you about setting one up. To qualify for one of these options, you'll generally need decent credit, a steady history of on-time payments on your first mortgage, and equity that's equal to more than 20% of the value of your home.

There are also a couple of other options, including one relatively new one. Depending on the interest rate on your first mortgage, you might consider a cash-out refinance with one of any number of mortgage banks that offer it. This option refinances your primary mortgage while also allowing you to take out some of your equity.

Or you might research a new product called a "home equity investment" or "equity sharing agreement," where you basically sell a portion of the equity in your property in exchange for a lump sum payment in the form of a loan. When it comes time to repay the loan, typically in ten years, you'll pay the amount of the lump sum plus a share of either the equity you've built in the property or the appreciation in the property since the loan was issued. Like a HELOC, the amount of money you can access is based on the value of your equity in an existing property. But compared with a HELOC, a home equity investment generally has lower credit requirements. Since we've never used this funding vehicle ourselves, we're not experts in it. But with the right research and due diligence, it could be a good option for some buyers.

And there's your $50k to acquire a property at a foreclosure auction.

Keep in mind that if the deal goes south, now you have more debt on your personal residence. If you can't repay that loan, now you could be looking at a foreclosure. Maybe using other people's money isn't such a bad idea after all?

CHOOSE YOUR OWN ADVENTURE

If you'd like to explore the options for
leveraging other people's money*, keep reading.*

*If using your own resources to make this investment seems
wicked risky and you're **not interested in leveraging other
people's money**, turn to page 305.*

*If you've now **got the money lined up** for a purchase, turn to page 121.*

LEVERAGING OTHER PEOPLE'S MONEY

If your funding strategy includes a third party, you're just lining up the lender at this point in the buying process. You're not necessarily lining up the actual funding, because ideally you're researching all your options well before you've identified the exact property you intend to buy. You need time to work with your lender and potentially jump through their hoops so they can approve a deal quickly when you bring one to them.

In other words, you're building a relationship. The gist of this first conversation goes something like, "Are you actively lending? I've got $10k of my own money. What I'm looking for is someone who can fund the purchase price, rehab cost, and six months of holding costs while I do the work. Let's say I find a three-bedroom, single-family house I can get for $50k. It's gonna need $50k in renovation. And once it's all fixed up, it's gonna be worth $150k. What do you need from me to be able to fund the deal? If I can bring you a deal, would you be able to fund that deal right away?"

You may think you need good credit and a healthy credit score to access third-party capital—but that's not necessarily true. In fact, there are several options for funding a real estate investment that rely instead on you and your credibility along with the fundamentals of the deal you're able to find.

THE MORE, THE BETTER

A learning moment for us was about having multiple relationships with banks. We needed funding for ten properties we had renovated and were ready to cash out. All of our money was tied up in the deals because at that time we were buying properties with cash. We would go to auctions and pay cash, so we had over a million dollars tied up in these properties. We also had more auctions coming up, but we didn't have any more capital to buy anything. So we went to our local bank to do a cash-out refinance like we had many times before.

Unexpectedly, they decided they wouldn't make commercial real estate loans specifically in this one town where we had all of our properties because the city started imposing surcharges and restrictions on REO properties. It was getting crazy, so the bank got scared. And all of a sudden, the banker just said "no." We were maybe thirty days into the refinancing process, and we had to start all over. The denial basically pushed us back over a month. Then we had to scramble to build a relationship with another bank quickly because we were already in the process of refinancing these properties.

Now we take our bankers and hard money lenders out to lunch more. We try to keep those relationships strong, even if we're not using them. The key is now we have open relationships with maybe seven or eight different banks. We might do most of our business with one bank for a while. But knowing that they might pivot or they might not meet our needs, it's good to have multiple options so we don't put ourselves in a corner like we did that one time.

We almost got into a big pickle because we had been banking with this bank for a while. We already had $6 or $7 million in loans with this one bank. We had built a really good relationship with them, so we trusted them. Which is all good and well, but banks are only there for themselves. They're not your friend. They might help you grow, but they're looking at their shareholders' bottom line, not your bottom line.

Once you have a short list of possible third-party sources of funding, you can get all their terms lined up so you can compare to find the best deal. The question is: Which one will work best for you?

CHOOSE YOUR OWN ADVENTURE

*If you plan to fund your purchase
with a **conventional mortgage**, keep reading.*

*If you'd like to explore ways to **partner with
another investor**, turn to page 102.*

*If you'd like to know more about getting funds from a **hard
money lender**, turn to page 105.*

*If you'd like to go a less conventional route and access funds from a
portfolio lender, turn to page 111.*

*If you're interested in our advice for funding your purchase with
private money, turn to page 116.*

***If you think your credit is a problem** for any of
these strategies, turn to page 119.*

CONVENTIONAL MORTGAGES

While there are many, many ways to fund a real estate purchase, one thing you probably can't do is get a conventional mortgage, for several reasons. First, most foreclosure contracts close within thirty days. In some judicial states, you might have as long as ninety days, but that's the exception and not the rule. Typically we see twenty to thirty days—so that's a very short window. And then basically you have to perform or the contract states you lose your deposit. If you fail to perform on the contract, the lienholder will take the second highest bidder—or whichever bidder is ready to perform. Once in a while, you might be able to request and receive an extension of the closing period for an extenuating reason, for instance because the bank hasn't finished its title work. But we don't recommend counting on it from a risk management standpoint, and certainly not because you don't have the financing to close.

The timeline is typically driven by the bank conducting the foreclosure and not you as the buyer. With a relatively short closing period, not to mention the other complications you might encounter (for example, an obstinate occupant), it's usually hard if not impossible to secure a conventional bank loan. Conventional bank loans typically take at least sixty days to close, and most conventional real estate deals take longer than that because of the time it takes to complete a title search, home inspections, environmental reviews, and all the other typical prepurchase research that happens after you sign a contract. With properties purchased at foreclosure auctions, there isn't any of that post-contract research because you've already agreed to buy the property as is, where is.

Second, many—not all, but many—properties are in significant disrepair such that a bank is going to be like, "Whoa, whoa, whoa. We can't lend on this." Maybe it's just very rundown, or maybe it doesn't have a roof or a working heating system. Maybe it has lead paint. If it's not habitable, it's generally not a property that a traditional bank will issue a mortgage against.

Moreover, by now you know that a lot of properties in foreclosure are occupied. It can be difficult if not impossible to get title insurance on an occupied property. And if you can't get title insurance, then you're not likely to get a conventional mortgage from a traditional bank.

Since you are legally obligated to close the deal once your bid has been accepted, you can now see why it's risky to plan on funding your purchase with a conventional loan. You're likely to end up either scrambling for another source of funds or losing your deposit.

That said, you may be able to get a short-term loan from another source and then refinance once you've remediated the issues that prevented you from getting a conventional loan in the first place. Or you could just use another strategy altogether.

CHOOSE YOUR OWN ADVENTURE

If you want to consider another option for **leveraging other people's money**, *turn back to page 95.*

If **none of the other options for leveraging other people's money** *are for you, turn to page 305.*

PARTNER WITH ANOTHER INVESTOR

Chances are, you probably already know someone interested in real estate investing and who might be a good partner for your new venture. You just have to find them.

The easiest way to find a partner to invest with—and something you should always be doing if you're really looking to get started on a real estate strategy—is social networking. Get the word out. Tell people, "Hey, I'm interested in [this]. I'm really interested in [that]." Almost every adult is now somewhat familiar with the concept of real estate flips, rentals, and investing to some trivial extent. Flip on the television and you're plagued by all these home makeover shows.

It's amazing how easy it is to strike up a conversation with someone who could turn out to be your financial partner. You can't go to a bar and have a beer without hearing a conversation three stools over about somebody who's a contractor or somebody who would love to buy a house and do a flip like they saw on TV. Go over to that guy and say, "Oh, you know what? I'm interested in doing the same thing. I'm thinking about [this], and what do you do? You've done a flip? That's really cool. How did you get your money?"

Or just attend a foreclosure auction. Most of the people there are investors, so you'll be able to build your network there if you're willing to start a conversation with the bidders. We've seen people partner right at a foreclosure auction. They knew each other a little bit beforehand, but they were at the auction and decided to partner up on one. So it's possible to do it right there on the fly. Realtors could also be a great resource. If you go to an open house for a flip, we practically guarantee that the realtor is a flipper themselves. Right there you've found someone who is a possible candidate to be a partner.

Believe it or not, banks are also a resource. We've made multiple connections with other investors by getting referrals from bankers. Especially if you talk to the commercial department in a bank that makes a lot of real estate investment loans, they're lending to investors. So guess what? They heard that Kevin Shippee is looking to partner up on a deal. Tell them, "I'm really looking to buy my next deal." Typically they'll get the word out among their other customers. We love working with local banks and local credit unions. You can usually build a personal relationship with their commercial loan officers.

And then there's social media. Join Facebook real estate groups; there are a million of them. Join landlord Meetup groups where you'll connect with a bunch of landlords who are almost always looking for deals. There are so many different investing groups out there. You can network to find contractors, lenders, contractors, workers—whatever it might be.

With any investor or partner, the more confidence you build, the more likely they are to do business with you. Show them you know what you're doing. If you show them you've taken the time to do your research and due diligence, they're going to be much more comfortable lending you money and trusting you. Their goal with their money is to keep it and grow it. They want to make sure that whoever they're partnering with or lending to will do the right thing by them. Giving them confidence that you will is key.

One way to do that is to have skin in the game by putting at least a little of your own money in the deal. When people have their own money in a deal, they tend to work harder than when they don't. If the deal starts going south, they're just losing their time and not their hard-earned money. We like our partners to have skin in the game for that reason. We want them to share the risk with us so that they will work their butts off to make sure their capital, and therefore my capital, is protected. If you're partnering with other people, it's gonna be easier to do any deal if you have at least a little money to put in. If you don't really have much money at all, partnering with someone is not impossible, but it's going to be harder.

But don't give up. You may still have a few options.

CHOOSE YOUR OWN ADVENTURE

*If you want to consider another option for **leveraging other people's money**, turn back to page 95.*

*If **none of the ideas for leveraging other people's money** are for you, turn to page 305.*

*If you've now **got the money lined up for the purchase**, turn to page 121.*

HARD MONEY LENDERS

If you don't have the money to get started on your own, hard money loans can be a great option. In fact, it's how we got started with our first rental property.

Hard money loans are generally short-term loans—typically from six months to two years—that carry higher interest rates than conventional bank loans, like ten percentage points more. While the interest rate is high, you figure the rate and the cost into your deal. A nice feature for real estate investors is that some loans carry interest-only payments, and some have no payments until the loan matures so that you can preserve your cash for the rehab. Then when you sell the property, the hard money loan gets paid first before any other investors because they take a first position on the property in terms of liens.

If you figure these costs into your deal and you stick to your estimated holding period, hard money can work really well. But if you don't follow through on your exit strategy, it *will* cost you. You don't want to stay long-term in a hard money loan because of the high interest rate. Some of the loans we've gotten also have to be renewed every year and charge an additional point or two at the renewal. So you do want to figure out your exit strategy before taking one on.

OH MY, LOOK AT THE TIME

We won a foreclosure auction for a very old farmhouse-style house in a nice little town in Massachusetts, and we leveraged hard money at 10% interest to do it. Then we just never got to the project. Like never even thought about it, really. We were running a mile a minute on our business, so it was almost four years before we actually started renovating the property. Then we spent an ungodly amount of time on it.

That's the thing to keep in mind with hard money. Often the loan will be for a one-year term. If you want to re-up it for longer, they charge you points. So not only did we pay 10% interest on the balance, but also at least two points every freaking year. We borrowed $200k. So 10% interest is $20k a year plus the two points, which is another $4k each year for four years. A total of about $100k. We essentially doubled our holding cost because we didn't follow our exit strategy properly. We should have been focusing on that.

Eventually we fixed the project up and sold the property, but we made nothing on that deal. We sold it for more than we owed, yes, but if you take the rehab and the holdings costs into consideration, we lost money.

The big lesson with hard money is that holding costs really add up quickly. And so, with hard money, have a good, quick exit strategy because that's how you'll keep your money.

We've actually made hard money loans to some of our friends in the business. One guy, a contractor, didn't allocate his time well either. He would sit on the projects. He would finish a project and then at the closing table, after we got paid back for the hard money loan, he'd walk away with almost nothing. He'd be like, "What the hell?"

And we'd say, "Dude. We keep telling you: You need to get the project done. You let it sit for a year. We didn't even charge you more points, but still it's expensive money. That's the cost of the loan." Because we often structure the hard money loans we make with no payments until the property sells, we think for some people out of sight is out of mind. If they're not actually being good stewards of their investments, they make almost no profit.

Hard money lenders can give you an opportunity to make a deal where you wouldn't have otherwise, which makes it worth factoring in the expense of the loan as part of the deal. If you were anticipating making $50k on the deal before figuring in your interest cost, now maybe you're making $40k. It's better than making nothing! And if your intention is to buy a property to owner-occupy, you might consider using a hard money loan to fund the initial purchase and give you time to refinance into a conventional mortgage. Hard money lenders can generally close in a week or two, much faster than a conventional loan that usually takes forty-five to sixty days, depending on the bank. As opposed to waiting for conventional financing, a hard money loan puts you in a position to get a great deal faster.

These loans work well to fund real estate investment strategies with shorter holding periods, including fix-and-flip and wholesaling. They work particularly well to fund the BRRRR method because hard money lenders are in a good position to help you not only with the "B" in the BRRRR method (the "Buy"), but also with the first "R" (which is "Rehab"). Hard money lenders are often willing to put in money for the rehab so you don't have to front all that cost yourself. You might be able to put down a deposit and borrow the rest of the rehab cost, for instance, and not be so out of pocket. It's a great way to leverage other people's money to grow your wealth.

The idea with the hard money loan is that you're not only going to have the money to buy the property, but also you're going to have the money ready and available to get started on the rehab right away. For the fix-and-flip buyer, you need to rehab and resell the property quickly to maximize your profit. For the BRRRR buyer, it's super-important to get through the rehab stage as quickly as possible so you can get to the refinance stage and get out of the hard money loan. You want to minimize the time in those first three stages—buy, rehab, rent—so that you get to the refinance and repeat stages as soon as possible. While hard money loans can sometimes be as long as two years, do you really want to pay 10%, 12%, 18% for two years? No. You don't. You want to ensure you're minimizing your costs, completing your steps through the process as quickly as possible. With the BRRRR strategy, and really with most real estate strategies, it's all about velocity.

One of the reasons to go to a hard money lender is timing. Another is credit, because you don't necessarily need good credit to get a loan from a hard money lender. A traditional bank looks at your credit and your income as criteria for making a loan. Instead, a hard money lender doesn't do that. They look at the value of the property and the fundamentals of the deal, to assess whether they can make money if the deal goes wrong and they have to take over the property.

If you find a great deal and take it to a hard money lender, they're more likely to lend than if you find a crappy deal. That's another protection for you as an investor, especially if you're new to the real estate game: If a hard money lender is willing to fund the deal you've found, you can feel confident that it's fundamentally solid. If the hard money lender tells you no, then it's probably not a good deal for you or for them. Most hard money lenders have a long history of flipping property, so they understand the market.

Another factor that a hard money lender will consider is your track record. If you've done a few flips, they'll feel more comfortable lending you money, which means you can negotiate better terms. If you're just starting out, you might consider partnering with someone else who's flipped a property or two before to build your own track record. But it's not a deal-killer if you don't. Remember: We got a hard money loan for our first deal, even after Matt had lost an investment property to foreclosure.

Once the hard money lender analyzes the deal on the property you've found, they'll tell you what they're willing to lend on it. Now you know your maximum bid, and you can go bid at the foreclosure auction with confidence. Let's say the maximum they're willing to lend you is $100k, and you win the bidding at $50k. You may be able to use the rest of the money to fund the rehab, and now you're off to the races.

There are many different ways to find a hard money lender, including just Googling "hard money lenders," joining Facebook groups and landlord associations, or even reaching out to your family or friends. Now you're combining hard money with private money—*that's* creative.

But wait, there's still more!

CHOOSE YOUR OWN ADVENTURE

*If you want to consider another option for **leveraging other people's money**, turn back to page 95.*

*If **none of the ideas for leveraging other people's money** are for you, turn to page 305.*

*If you've now **got the money lined up for the purchase**, turn to page 121.*

PORTFOLIO LENDERS

Portfolio lenders, also known as manual underwriters, are banks that keep their loans in-house instead of selling them off to the secondary market where they have to follow government and other guidelines for lending. Instead, they develop and follow their own guidelines for lending. Often they're local banks as opposed to large, national banks. As a result, they tend to have a lot more flexibility than other banks, and they're often much-more investor friendly. The other great thing is they tend to approve loans much quicker because they don't have to follow the underwriting guidelines of the secondary market such as Fannie Mae and FHA.

One of the reasons they can be really beneficial to a real estate investor is that, once you have a relationship with them, they can often be more creative when they underwrite loans. If you think you might start buying properties at foreclosure auctions as a regular investment, developing a relationship with a portfolio lender could be a smart way to go. There's a big BUT, though: If you're looking to use a portfolio lender to fund a purchase from a foreclosure auction, you need to have an established relationship that gives you a little pull because of the accelerated closing periods for many foreclosure auction sales.

Because of the nonconforming nature of these loans, typically you pay a slightly higher interest rate. However, you might also get access to more flexible loan products, like no doc or bank statement loans, which are made based on the balances on your bank statements as opposed to income on your tax returns. For this reason, bank statement loans are often an attractive option for small business owners.

To find a portfolio lender, call the commercial departments of the banks and credit unions in your area and ask if they do any portfolio lending. Some will, some won't. In our area quite a few credit unions do portfolio lending.

JUST IN TIME

We once used a portfolio lender for a $2.2 million purchase at a foreclosure auction. We didn't have the money ourselves at the time, so we had to explore all the avenues for pulling funds together from the available sources.

We could have gotten hard money, which would have cost us 12% interest plus almost two points. That would've been a lot of money on $2.2 million. We considered private money, but we were already over-leveraged on the private money we had access to, so we would have had to either go hat in hand to them or find new people. And the cost would probably have been 10% interest plus one point—still pretty expensive on $2.2 million. So the last avenue was a portfolio lender, a local credit union to be exact, who offered us a loan rate of just over 4%.

It was risky, though, because we had to close in thirty days from the date of the auction or forfeit our $200k deposit. The deposit was large because the purchase price was large. So, hell, we didn't want to lose that money. But we talked to a local credit union that's a portfolio lender, which means they actually underwrite their loans in-house. They don't sell the loans on the secondary mortgage market. They probably do sell some conventional mortgage loans on the secondary market, but they do not sell most of their investor loans. That's really advantageous to investors like us because it means their loans don't have to conform with federal loan guidelines and loan limits. The portfolio lender can create their own guidelines, and often they can be a little bit more creative with their loans. They might charge a slightly higher interest rate, but they might be a lot more creative on the back end too.

We needed a closing in thirty days, but the credit union's normal closing timeline on commercial real estate loans was sixty days because their due diligence included an environmental study. The clock started ticking on the day of the auction, and we started pushing. We quickly got the environmental report. Then we talked to the lender. We kept telling them, "We need to close in thirty days, thirty days, thirty days, thirty days."

Five days before the thirty days were up, we knew we weren't going to make it. The credit union needed another week. In desperation, we took a big risk: We went back to the auction house and the lawyer for the bank and said, "Hey, we're so close. Can we get an extension of two weeks for the closing?"

They said, "Okay, but you have to put up another $20k for the deposit."

On the one hand, whew. On the other, that ups our risk of losing an even bigger deposit. But we felt very solid that we could close within the additional two weeks, so we paid it.

The loan closed a little over a week later. The deal got done.

That was not easy. It was a lot of risk because banks typically don't move that fast. The only reason why the loan got processed in record time was that the credit union really wanted it for their portfolio. They knew us. At this point we'd been in business fourteen years. The LTV on the deal was massive because the property was worth close to $5 million, and we bought it for $2 million. That's very low risk from the lender's perspective. It also helped a lot that one of our business partners golfs with the company's higher-ups, so he had personal relationships that helped when it came time to get approval from the board of directors. So the stars aligned—but it was close.

Again, it is not a strategy for the faint of heart. Can it be done? We made it happen. But it's not something we want to do on a regular basis.

Especially if you're just getting started in real estate investing, working with a portfolio lender may not be the first or easiest path to funding an acquisition through a foreclosure auction. But don't give up! There are still quite a few other funding strategies. Sometimes it just requires some creativity.

CHOOSE YOUR OWN ADVENTURE

*If you want to consider another option for **leveraging other people's money**, turn back to page 95.*

*If **none of the ideas for leveraging other people's money** are for you, turn to page 305.*

*If you've now **got the money lined up** for the purchase, turn to page 121.*

PRIVATE MONEY

Private money is a friend or family member with money to invest. Only some people out there are living paycheck to paycheck. A lot of people we hear from through our YouTube channel think everyone is struggling. We get a lot of comments like, "I can't believe this video, when everybody I know is struggling. Everybody is struggling! Nobody has any money."

But the reality is there are people with *boats* out there. There are people with fine sports cars. There are always people buying investment property. So not *everyone* is struggling, dude. Not everybody is broke as a joke. And trust us, you can't judge how much money someone has to invest from the car they drive. Your grandma may drive an old Honda Civic or 2008 Toyota Prius while she keeps $50k under a mattress that she'd be willing to lend you on the right deal.

So, believe it or not, more people out there aren't struggling and may have $100k to invest in your plan. To those people, Kev would like to say that his birthday is in August, and Matt's is in February. Kev's a size medium, and he likes blue, but orange is great too.

You may know somebody with money to invest and a good reason to put money in real estate. Maybe they don't want all their money in the stock market, so they're even willing to tap their own 401(k). We've had a few investors who've given us millions of dollars because they didn't want to keep it in the market. They were happy to get a preferred return with us of 10% when we started working together. Some of them now take a consistent 8%, as opposed to the market where the returns are volatile. They're happy with an 8% return in exchange for not having to worry about the ups and downs of the stock market.

Maybe someone you know has money but no time, and they would love to get into real estate with a go-getter. While not everyone is fortunate enough to have family members or friends with money to lend, many do. Some people are born into money. Many times people have money to lend not because they hit a scratch ticket, but because they made smart decisions, they analyzed things, they worked, and they didn't take frivolous risks or do silly things with their money. They didn't just throw it around. They were careful and earned it and preserved it and made wise choices with it. They had the good sense and good fortune to build a nest egg.

Talk to them just like you would a bank or any investor. Present them with information about why this opportunity you're offering is a good choice for them, why it's a safe choice for them, why you think you're going to be successful, and why their money is going to be safe in your hands. In this conversation, don't treat them as your Uncle Charlie. Treat them instead as a wealthy investor who you're fortunate to have access to. The fact that he's Uncle Charlie just gets you a spot at the table. It's a personal relationship that can lead to a business partnership, but treat them as a business partner, not as Uncle Charlie. From there you have to treat the person like any other smart, professional investor to whom you're presenting your business plan.

CHOOSE YOUR OWN ADVENTURE

If you want to consider another option for **leveraging other people's money**, *turn back to page 95.*

If **none of the ideas for leveraging other people's money** *are for you, turn to page 305.*

If you've now **got the money lined up** *for the purchase, turn to page 121.*

IF YOU THINK YOUR CREDIT IS A PROBLEM

Believe it or not, there are quite a few options for pulling together money even if your credit history isn't great. Remember our advice about being bold and ballsy? Well, this is where it matters. Kev hears from people all the time on his TikTok channel who complain about all the reasons they can't do what we've done. To that we say, "Don't tell us why you can't. Tell us why you *can*."

We were just out of college when we started buying real estate, and Matt had just come through a foreclosure on a rental property. We didn't let that stop us—and you don't have to let it stop you.

Sometimes the solution is just a matter of time. Credit heals faster than a lot of people think. Six months could make a massive difference in your credit score in terms of getting a loan approval for whatever you're looking at. So maybe it's not that you can't do it. It's just that you can't do it until a few months from now. Take the time and make an effort to understand why your credit score is what it is, and then make a plan to improve it.

Or—sometimes the solution is a matter of effort. Do some homework on these options for accessing capital to fund your purchase, which don't necessarily rely on your credit history.

CHOOSE YOUR OWN ADVENTURE

*To look at creative options for **tapping your own resources**, turn to page 91.*

*To learn more about working with a **hard money lender** like we do, turn to page 105.*

*If you'd like our advice for accessing **private money**, turn to page 116.*

CHAPTER 5

MAKE A GAME PLAN

We have a game plan for every foreclosure we bid on. At this point in our business we do minor rehab, for instance, but if a property is in really bad condition, then we're most likely going to flip it to someone else who'll rehab it. We also source houses for some of our investors, and then our work is to find foreclosures to flip to them. We'll just wholesale it right to the investor. We have a list of buyers. When we find a house that meets their criteria, we call them up. "Hey, Mr. Investor. I just found this single-family home in the area you like, with a rehab budget of $60k. You should be able to make $50k profit." We give them a clean title. Sometimes we'll even give them a hard money loan to purchase and rehab it. We're a one-stop shop for a handful of real estate investors. Since we use a handful of strategies to maximize the profit on our real estate investments, we make sure that we're clear on the game plan for every property we buy before we buy it.

It's important to know our game plan before the auction because our intention can impact our maximum allowable offer (MAO), choice of financing, optimal holding period, and cash flow projections. Whether we plan to fix-and-flip, wholesale or buy-and-hold changes our definition of a "good deal." It even changes how we run the numbers to analyze the deal. Then we look at the deal from the opposite direction too: We run the numbers and then figure out which bucket the deal might fit in. Every deal is going to be different. If it's a buy-and-hold, we want to make at least a 15% cash-on-cash return annually. For a fix-and-flip, we need to make a 40% return on our investment, while our ROI can be a fraction of that if we're wholesaling.

Other bidders at foreclosure auctions are making the same calculations based on their own intentions, so it's a good idea to go in with an understanding of how a bidder's intention will impact the amount they are willing to bid. In general, a homebuyer will be the most competitive bidder because they don't have to include a profit margin in their calculations, followed by a long-term investment buyer, followed by flippers and wholesalers, each of whom is looking at a slightly different set of assumptions when calculating their maximum bid (more on that later).

That's another reason it's a good idea to have a game plan before you head to the auction: It helps mitigate the risk of getting too excited or too emotionally invested at the auction and losing sight of the MAO, which is based on *your* specific plans for the property.

Before you can make a good game plan, you have to know what your expectation is for the property and the path you intend to take to realize it. If your path includes renovating it, then you can analyze the best way to get the rehab done. It's either "I have the time to do the renovation work and will put in the time myself. I'm good at it and I want to do that. It'll be fun for me." Or it's "I want to continue focusing on my full-time job and hang out with my family. So I'm going to budget enough money and run my numbers on the assumption that I'll hire a contractor to do the renovation work; or my cousin can do it affordably, way less than if I were to hire a guy out of the Yellow Pages" (if that's still even still a thing).

As soon as you own the property, your holding costs start adding up. One key way to maximize your profit is to minimize your holding costs and get to the point where the property is either producing cash flow or fulfilling its intended purpose as quickly as you can. You want to make as many decisions as possible about what you're going to do and how you're going to do it *before* the deed is in your hands.

WHERE'S THE EXIT?

We have a property now that we're still trying to sell.

We went to the first auction for it sometime in 2019. Matt was there, along with one other bidder. It was an occupied house with farm animals around it, but Matt thought they were on a separate property. It was weird. We ran our numbers, calculated the ARV at $500k, and calculated our MAO. Then he won the bidding. For some reason, maybe a title issue, the bank canceled the bid, returned our deposit, and rehosted the auction. This time no one else was there. Matt was the only bidder. He bid the same amount as the first time, $225k, and won the auction again.

We still felt it was a really good deal. Matt knocked on the door after winning the auction because he knew it was occupied. Someone came to the door and showed him around the place a little bit. He got a couple of phone numbers and then as usual, handed it off to Kev. And, of course, our dynamic is such that the handoff was like, "Hahaha! Good luck, Kev. This is a mess, but we also need it resolved right away." Because this one was definitely expensive.

As soon as we closed on it after the foreclosure auction, we were out there urgently trying to empty it. It was condemnable. None of it was up to code. The people living in it had wiring in their shower from their bathroom ceiling fan. They had opened it up and spliced the wires for power, and then ran one of the wires to a little light fixture that was dangling over their shower rod. That's how they had light in their bathroom. There was no heat in the place whatsoever. They were using space heaters rigged up however they could. There were holes in all the walls and all the typical features of a shack of a place. They had just insane mold; mold is such an overblown thing, but still.

Kev had to go there to aggressively negotiate with occupants to GTFO. He figured out that it was basically used as a rooming house, so several unrelated people or households were living in different bedrooms. Some guy kept coming around proclaiming himself the property manager. The previous owners lived out of state. The property manager guy would come around and collect rents from the other people living there, and all the money was just going right to him. He would strong-arm them and they'd cough up a few hundred bucks here and there. That was enough to support his habit. Turns out he was actually making meth there at one point.

So Kev started rounding people up. It's a bit of a drive from where he lives, but he was going out there quite a few times to catch all the different people at whatever time he could catch them. Then he started negotiating cash-for-keys offers with them. It was taking a lot of time, and we needed them off the property right away because it was condemnable, and if something bad were to happen, we'd be liable for it.

We had been trying to get the city to condemn the property way before we took ownership of it, because then we wouldn't have had to deal with all rando people. If the city had condemned it, the property would have been the old owner's problem. The messed up thing is once they found out we won that first auction, the city kept reaching out to us saying, "Oh great, I'm glad you guys are involved. What's your plan? Are you going to get these people cleared out? Are you going to fix this place up?"

We were like, "We're not even the owners yet. All we did was win an auction. So, since you know that there are all these atrocious conditions on the property, what are you going to do? Aren't you condemning it?" We started aggressively contacting the city and trying to get them to do something with it before we took ownership. They just never did, for whatever reason.

So, we took ownership. And Kev started corralling the occupants and making cash-for-keys deals, some of which included time in a hotel because we couldn't let them live on the property in that condition. Kev booked motel rooms and told them, "Listen, I got you four or five days over here at this motel. Here's some money in your hand so you can figure out where you're going to go."

Kev would work a deal with one, and then they'd talk to someone else he'd already negotiated with. Then they'd renege on the deal and demand more money. Then other people started showing up saying, "Oh, well, we actually live here too. We need cash for keys." One woman had all her animals on the property, but didn't live there. Then all of a sudden she came back and said, "Actually, I do live here."

She had a cat and a dog and like forty other animals, every other animal you could possibly imagine was there. There was a bull. She had goats. There were tons of horses. There were cows. They had all encroached across the property line. Allegedly, the owner of the adjacent property gave her permission to keep the animals there. Then she set up fences that encroached onto our property. That should have been an easy fix: "Move your fences, move your animals, move everything over. Here are a couple hundred bucks." But then she put her hand out for more money claiming she lived in the house too. Finally, Kev was like, "Okay, fine. Here's $500. Sign off on this document saying you don't live here."

It would have cost us thousands and months to evict her, so it was worth giving her $500 just to put an end to the situation. We ended up getting everyone out for a total of maybe a few grand and a few nights in motels here and there.

We had one of our maintenance guys in and out of there quite a bit during this time, and he learned one of the people had something going on with goats. One of the randos proclaimed himself to be "onsite maintenance," and he also helped with the farm animals. When our guy was there one day to inspect the smoke detectors, the Onsite Maintenance Guy still hadn't left. So our guy knocks, "Knock, knock, knock." No answer.

He called us for permission to enter anyway, and we told him to go on inside since the appointment was scheduled and we had to check the smoke detectors. While he's in the kitchen area, he hears this loud, squeaking noise coming from the back bedroom area. It sounded like a goat getting hurt. All of a sudden, Onsite Maintenance Guy comes out from the back room, and our guy can see there are goats in Onsite Maintenance Guy's bedroom. He didn't ask any other questions. He just got the freak outta there.

Since then we've been holding onto the property for two years, burning $2k a month, unable to move it. We should have had a game plan for what we were going to do. It was an odd property. It was bordering on a conservation area, and it was farm-zoned. It's a simple house. The roof was newer. There's no basement. So we thought the rehab couldn't be that bad. We thought we could easily wholesale it. But this is where we should have done more due diligence.

We should have talked to the town more and figured out some things in advance. We knew that the title was questionable, but we got that resolved. We found out it has a shared well. And then there are multiple easements with the neighbor that aren't for the life of the property. They're for just five years or something like that. So we've had multiple buyers, but they've all talked to this neighbor who scares them off. We've now lost three deals, and we're in the middle of one more. The neighbor needs to sign off that his easement is still good, or we'll probably lose this buyer as well.

Our other exit strategy option at this point is to renovate the property ourselves and then sell it. But that's going to be very hard. There are still farm animals behind the house on the property that we don't own, and there's a massive metal structure that's twenty-five feet tall. What are we going to do with that, put up a thirty-foot fence to hide it? People paying good money for this kind of a place will not want that kind of eyesore bordering the property, or sad farm animals owned by someone who doesn't take care of them, or this contentious neighbor.

If a property has enough value in it relative to what you buy it for, you can survive having to pivot your strategy. In this case, we bought it so cheap relative to market value that it was hard to screw up. We're finding a way to screw it up because of our holding costs while we figure out what to do with it. We leveraged hard money on this purchase. So we've been paying 10% on that money every year for three years plus two points. We refinance it every year that we haven't sold it, and we pay two points to refinance it. So basically, the profit margin just keeps getting smaller and smaller and smaller.

We should have had a plan for it before we bid on the sucker. And now because we didn't, we're still trying to figure out who's going to buy it. If we can get our act together now, the market could save us. The market went up and up and up while we held it, so appreciation will cover all the mistakes we made. Thank God we made the mistake on the upswing of a market. If we made that same mistake now, we could really be in trouble.

When you've thought through your assumptions for the entire process you plan to follow, you can anticipate the hurdles and then plan on how you're going to get around those hurdles. We can't say this enough: Don't neglect this part of the process. We've seen it where people have gotten a property under contract and have no idea where to go next. Don't let that be you. Be clear on your intentions for the property, and understand how your intentions shape your game plan.

CHOOSE YOUR OWN ADVENTURE

If you intend to **acquire a property to owner-occupy**, *turn the page.*

If you intend to **acquire a property to buy-and-hold for investment***, turn to page 132.*

If you intend to **acquire a property to flip***, turn to page 140.*

ACQUIRE A PROPERTY TO OWNER-OCCUPY

If you're looking to owner-occupy, the auction process is a whole different ball game for you than it is for investors because that's your only exit strategy. All you need to know is what you can afford to buy, what you're willing to afford to buy, and if it's a house that meets your needs. Owner-occupants don't necessarily need as much of a game plan as other buyers.

Buyers who intend to own and occupy a property are the most competitive bidders at a foreclosure auction, because they're not looking for the same spread on their investment as investors. A homebuyer will always pay more than we will because they're looking for a home, and we're looking for a return on our investment. They're just looking at getting a deal on maybe a fixer-upper—probably a fixer-upper. If they intend to buy a property to live in and then house-hack it, they may even be able to bid a little more than the typical owner-occupier if they figure the additional cash flow into their funding assumptions.

We regularly help homebuyers we run into at foreclosure auctions if we've decided not to bid. If we see a homebuyer at an auction who we're confident is not a real estate investor, we may decide not to bid against them because we generally know we can't win. So if we're not willing to buy, we'll give a homebuyer honest feedback and help guide them through the process a little bit just because we don't want to see them get screwed.

We were interested in this one house that turned out to need a new septic system, which could cost $30k. We knew there was also a roughly $10k lien for back taxes. Once Matt got to the house and saw the condition of it, he knew it wasn't for us. But a potential homeowner at the auction was super-interested. They'd been trying to get a house for a really long time and it was in an area they wanted, so they were willing to bid pretty high.

Matt helped educate them, like, "Just so you know, I'm not going to bid. I'm not interested in buying it, so I'm not your competition. But you need to be mindful that the D-box in the electrical system is shot. The leach field in the septic system needs to be replaced. And if you win, you're going to have to pay the back taxes as well. So make sure you take that into consideration when you're bidding." We don't know how many professional buyers will give homebuyers that kind of advice, but we've certainly done it.

CHOOSE YOUR OWN ADVENTURE

*If you want to learn how **buying and holding** for investment impacts your game plan, turn the page.*

*If you want to learn how **flipping the property** impacts your game plan, turn to page 140.*

*If you're ready to **roll up your sleeves**, turn to page 147.*

ACQUIRING A PROPERTY TO BUY-AND-HOLD FOR INVESTMENT

If our intention were to buy and hold for use as a rental, our maximum bid would be probably lower than if we were buying a house to live in. If one of us were buying a house for our family as a place to raise our kids and we found a perfect one in a good school system, then we wouldn't mind paying a little more for it than we pay for our investment properties. A lot of buyers will pay a little bit more to live in a stylish house in that perfect neighborhood with good schools. But that's not the main consideration when buying a rental property for investment.

For a rental, the primary consideration is whether the property can more than support itself from the income it will generate. We don't want to buy something, fix it up, and then have our total cost be more than what the rents will cover in cash flow. Investors generally don't want to buy a property and then rent it out and deal with the headache of tenants and property management only to have the rental income *just* cover the property's expenses. They want the expenses of the property covered *plus* a few hundred bucks per unit positive so they earn some income every month while they're paying the mortgage down over thirty years.

If we run our numbers to calculate our MAO and figure out that we're going to make only $10 per tenant in profit every month after covering all our expenses including the debt on the property, we probably won't bid at the auction because it seems like a whole lot of pain for not a whole lot of reward if we win. Sure, we may own a house free and clear in thirty years, but as investors, we're generally not looking for a return thirty years down the road.

PLAN FOR THE LTR, BANK ON THE STR

If you're buying a property as a short-term rental (STR), you *could* pay a higher price based on your higher anticipated cash flows relative to a long-term rental (LTR)—but what happens if things change? You don't have a way to pivot the property.

We've seen people bidding up the price of rental properties based on an assumption that the higher short-term rental rates support a higher price. The problem we see is that they're backing themselves into a corner. What happens when the city passes an ordinance two years into your thirty-year mortgage that severely limits or even bans STRs? Or what happens if the STR market changes or dries up? If you base your purchase price on that market, then you don't have many ways you can pivot to ensure that the income from the property covers its expenses.

We always suggest having a backup plan. For example, it's easy to base your bid on an assumption of the income the property can generate as a long-term rental and then say, "Hey, you know what? I can make way more money, at least for now, using it as an STR." So buy it based on the long-term rental cash flows, and then rake in the extra income from renting it short-term. But you can't do it the other way around.

CHOOSE YOUR OWN ADVENTURE

*If you want to learn how **acquiring a property to owner-occupy** impacts your game plan, turn back to page 130.*

*If you want to learn how **acquiring a property to flip** impacts your game plan, turn to page 140.*

*If you're ready to **roll up your sleeves**, turn to page 147.*

BRRRR! IT'S GOLD!

We started off using the BRRRR strategy before it was a thing, and we thought we were blazing a new path. And then Brandon Turner decided to coin the phrase and took all the credit.

Step 1: Buy

The first letter is "B," which stands for Buy. Now, what are you buying? You're buying a distressed or undervalued property, in this case a foreclosure property. That's the key part of it: buying the property right. You want to buy a property with upside potential so you can create value. That's why buying a property at a foreclosure auction is such a great opportunity, and an ideal way to launch this strategy, because more often than not, a foreclosure auction is where you can get a very good deal.

Step 2: Rehab

The second letter is "R," which stands for Rehab. This is where you're building value in the property, whether it's through sweat equity or by hiring contractors to do the work, to increase your equity in the property. The whole idea is that you're making significant improvements for less than the improvements are worth. So if you're going to create $75k of value in the rehab, you're doing it at a fraction of that cost.

There are various ways to do that, so you want to look at the things that add *the most* value—for instance, popping on a roof. The top things to build value in a rental property would be the big things like roofs, heating systems, electrical, water lines, kitchens, baths, flooring, and even just paint. Simply painting a property is low-cost, but it can make such a difference in the perceived value. You want to stay away from renovating things that have very little return on your costs. Over-renovating a kitchen or a bathroom or other property elements where you're investing $20k but only getting $20k in value back is not a smart way to invest your money.

Then you're going to hire contractors you can work well with and get the cost down. Whereas maybe someone else would replace the roof for $20k, you're able to get it done for $12k. That same idea applies to all the different aspects of the property. If you need to do plumbing or electrical work, chances are you're not able or inclined to do that work yourself. In that case, you want to staff it out to people who can do it at a very discounted price for you.

To figure out the expectations for your market, go on Zillow, Trulia, Realtor.com, Redfin, and other real estate sites to see what fixtures and finishes other properties in your market have. If they all have granite, then you will want to put in granite. But if they all have laminate, then putting in granite might not make the most sense; it might not bring you that extra value. You really have to look at what's out there and compare. Doing your rehab in the most cost-effective way is the chief point here.

Step 3: Rent

So you've rehabbed the property, and it's beautiful. Now what do you do? Now you're going to rent it out. You're going to find a great, qualified tenant who you can get maximum value for that unit. Renting the property out is incredibly important because it's going to help you in the later stage, the next "R." You need to have a great lease with a very favorable rental rate on this property so you can use that rental as income to help you qualify for the next upcoming "R."

So, how do you go about finding a great tenant? There are a lot of great ways, honestly. You can post something on Facebook Marketplace. You can put in minimal work to make an ad and have people go through basic steps to inquire about it and pass a screening process. If you haven't already, find a great property manager; they can do a lot of this for you. Once you have the property ready, they'll go out and market it—take photos, shoot professional drone footage, create 3D tours, all that kind of stuff—to attract the best tenant. They're going to use their screening process that they've taken years to develop, and they'll handle that all for you. They'll charge a fee for doing this, but you have to decide if that fee is important enough to forgo or not.

We suggest there are many other things that come with a professional management company that help protect you. The number one thing you have to worry about if you're inexperienced with rentals is a discrimination situation. There are a lot of things to know from a legal standpoint about the application and the tenant-screening processes. For a rookie who is unfamiliar with this stuff, you may be inviting disaster. The most innocuous thing in a marketing ad could result in a discrimination suit. If you're not well versed in this area, we highly recommend finding a property management company like ourselves to work with you.

Many people find it well worth their time and money because screening tenants, showing a property, getting everybody on-boarded—it's very time-consuming. Even just showing an apartment can be incredibly frustrating because, if you haven't screened them properly, many people simply don't show up for the showings you've taken time to schedule.

Step 4: Refinance

The third "R" is Refinance. Now you're going to go out, talk to a bunch of different banks, and get the best rate possible by pitting them against each other for what's called a "cash-out refinance." They're going to look at your loan-to-value (LTV). That is, the amount of money you want to borrow relative to the equity you have in the property. Different banks will have different LTV thresholds at different times of the economic cycle. For example, if they're talking about a 70% LTV and the value of the property is $100k, they're going to give you a mortgage of $70k. That's $70k you can pull out of the property to fund your next deal.

Let's say you bought the property and renovated it with the cash you borrowed from your IRA so you're out $60k: You bought the property for $40k and you put $20k into it. And now the bank sends out an appraiser who says, "Wow. You did such a great job. You got it rented out. It's now worth $100k." The bank hands you a check for $70k, which means you get all your money back *plus* an extra $10k that's tax-free *and* you still have $30k of equity in the property. You have $10k more than you started with because you bought an undervalued property, put sweat equity into it, and increased its equity.

It's a simple process, but it's not easy, and not everybody knows about it.

Step 5: Repeat

The last "R" stands for Repeat, as in repeating the process. Based on our example, you have $10k in extra cash in hand and $30k in equity. Why not take the cash and do it again by buying another property? You have a great property that's cash flowing, so why wouldn't you want to do this another ten, twenty, or thirty times?

The whole time you're going through the rest of the process after the "B," you have to be ready to farm to find another "B," another target property to buy. And this is one of the reasons why you need to build a great team. If you have a great wholesaler or someone else, a realtor or someone who is looking out for that next property, you're just focusing on hiring the contractors and managing the BRRR process on the first property you bought, talking with the banks, playing puppet master so that you can keep this ball rolling over and over again and do what we did until we got to five hundred rental units. In our example, we're talking about hiring a property manager, which does cost you money out of the monthly rent and maybe maintenance. But many people find it worthwhile because you get to keep focusing on the bigger picture and bigger dollars of doing these projects over and over and over.

ACQUIRE A PROPERTY TO FLIP

If your exit strategy is to flip the home that you plan to buy at a foreclosure auction, you have to know in advance what you'll be comfortable with in terms of return on investment. Ask yourself, "If I buy the property for $X, what kind of percent return do I want?" For example, if you're into the property for $200k, do you need a 30% return or $60k before commissions and taxes, etc.? We know investors who are comfortable with a 10% or 15% return. Maybe they have workers to pay, and are willing to take a slimmer profit when work is slow because they have to keep money coming in just to cover their costs. It may make sense for some buyers in certain situations. But to us, that seems crazy because it's so risky to operate with such thin margins. You can lose your shirt if anything goes wrong or if any of your assumptions were wrong. We require a 30% return on properties we buy.

Now, with mortgage rates at their highest since 2008, flipping has become harder and riskier. Generally speaking, every 1% increase in interest rates lowers people's purchasing power 6-10%. It may take a little time for the market to adjust, but you almost always see a 6-10% decrease in property values for every hundred basis points or a 1% increase in interest rates. If you're in the middle of a flip that you purchased with the expectation of a 15% return and interest rates rise during your holding period, you could be down to a 5% return by the time you're ready to sell it—and that's if everything else about the property goes as expected. Which it never does.

CHOOSE YOUR OWN ADVENTURE

*If you want to learn how **acquiring a property to owner-occupy** impacts your game plan, turn back to page 130.*

*If you want to learn how **acquiring a property buy-and-hold for investment** impacts your game plan, turn back to page 132.*

*If you're ready to **roll up your sleeves**, turn to page 147.*

FLIPPING 101

You can find people interested in buying properties in any market, which means flipping can work in any market if you have the right strategy and you buy at the right price.

Retail Flipping

Retail flipping is when you are fully renovating a property to make it move-in ready. Typically, you upgrade the property to today's standards, maybe adding granite, redoing the flooring, and repainting. If it needs a new roof, you put on a new roof. You upgrade the kitchen and heating system. The goal when you're done is to list the property for the retail buyer rather than an investor in distressed properties. You might work with a realtor to put it on the Multiple Listing Service (MLS) and all the retail home websites like Zillow, Redfin, and Trulia.

Typically, retail flipping is riskier during the down phase of a real estate market. At the same time, it can still be done if you're buying the property for less than market value. The problem is, you don't want to catch a falling knife. If you get properties under market value, renovate them in a timely fashion, and then sell them under market value, you can still make money. Real estate is an inefficient market; there's a lag between falling demand and falling prices. It's not like the stock market or crypto where you can lose trillions of dollars in a second. It will take months for prices to fall. There's a lot of human sentiment behind it and a lot of moving parts related to supply, demand, interest rates, inflation rates, etc. So, retail flipping can work in a downmarket; you just have to be careful.

In an upmarket, making money on retail flipping is simple: You buy a property and by the time you sell it, it's worth more than what you thought it would be worth when you bought it. Upmarkets are a very good time for the retail flipping strategy. In a downmarket, you don't want to get caught at the top of the cycle. There will be a point when you're buying property and then it's worth less than you thought it would be by the time you sell it. As long as you maintain good margins, you can maybe get out without losing your shirt. The key is to get out at the right time. In a downmarket, we'll sometimes sell our flips for less than we think we should just so we can undercut the market. We just get out.

Wholesale Flipping

Wholesale flipping is a different story, because there's very limited risk. As long as you can find a wholesale buyer before you commit to the deal, you can make money. The issue might be that there are fewer active buyers of all kinds in a downmarket, including wholesale buyers. Even some wholesalers are saying, "In this market, I'm going to wait."

Wholesaling property is a great way to make money on foreclosed properties when you don't have the time, skill, money, or inclination to do a rehab. In real estate, wholesaling means finding and buying a distressed property for sale and immediately flipping it to another buyer. You're basically the middleman for buyers—mostly investors—who, for whatever reason, don't want to spend their time finding properties.

Here's how it works. The first step is finding a property that needs significant rehab. Next, you're going to get the property under contract as the buyer. Then you're going to either sell the contract or do what's called a "double-close," which is when you sell the property at the same time that you buy it. There's basically just an exchange of paperwork. If you're assigning the contract, the contract you've written up says you're either buying it or you're going to assign it to someone else who is going to buy it. So now you need to find someone who wants to buy a house fast.

If you haven't already built your buyer's list, there are a couple of key ways to build one. First, you should create the list as you're looking for properties to buy. One of the ways to do that is to attend your local real estate Meetup groups. Find out who's buying properties in your area. The social aspect of this is very important. Start making acquaintances, start making friends, start hanging out with people in the real estate world. Join real estate-oriented Facebook groups like crazy. Join real estate investor groups in your area. Start getting your name out there a little bit. Once you've found a property you want to wholesale, post it on Facebook and say, "DM me." You're going to get a ton of DMs. Trust us.

Most importantly, start keeping track of the names of the people who tell you they're interested in acquiring a house and maybe doing a flip someday. Create a Google Doc or way to keep track of their information, including what kind of property they're interested in, whether it's single-family or multifamily, etc. Keep track of their contact info, including their names and telephone numbers.

As soon as you've found a property that could match the interest of someone on your list, you should be blowing up that buyer's phone. You want to give them as much head's up and time to decide as you possibly can. You want to get the word out to as many different buyers as possible, so that you can hopefully get competing offers: "Hey, Joe Investor. Guess what? I just got this single-family home in that area you like. Rehab budget $60K. You should be able to make $40k-$50k profit."

Matt keeps a preferred buyer's list of the people we sell to regularly. When he finds a property that fits their profiles, he goes to them first. They've done business with us, they know our deals work for them, and we know they can close on the deal. And why wouldn't we treat our best customers the best? We know they're going to perform, and they know we're going to deliver exactly what they're looking to buy with accurate ARVs; reasonable rehab estimates; and vacant, cleaned out, no muss, no fuss properties with marketable titles. And we always talk to multiple people, not just the one or two who are always game to buy a property. Why? First, because it's good for us when there's a bidding war, and second, because we want to get the deal done quickly so we can move on. Remember, velocity is your friend with real estate investing.

If they find out what you bought the property for at auction, be honest and direct about your own profit in the deal. Say, "This is the fee I'm making." Being honest and open is not a bad policy at all. Everybody thinks that if the buyer in a wholesale deal knows you're making money on a property you're flipping to them, they're going to say, "That's not fair! You're not doing anything to earn that money!" But that's not how this strategy works whatsoever.

Most buyers know that you as the wholesaler will make a fee as the middleman. Why would they want to pay someone a fee? Because their time is valuable. Maybe they have the renovation skills, the ability to get a renovation up and running, and then get the property resold quickly, and that's what they're great at. But they're not so great at sourcing and negotiating for the properties they rehab. You are. They recognize what you're great at, and they're willing to pay for that service. If they're happy to make $30k, $40k, or whatever profit they typically make, they're not going to turn down a deal where they can make money just because you're also making money. That wouldn't make any sense.

CHAPTER 6

BUYER BEWARE

Due diligence is the difference between making a successful purchase at a foreclosure auction and buying an absolute train wreck of a property that will haunt you forever—and is maybe haunted itself. The more due diligence you have, the safer the investment can be. Given how inherently risky the process is, it's really important to reduce any risk factors if at all possible. No matter what you do, you can never mitigate all the risks, but the goal of any investor is to mitigate as much risk as possible.

When it comes to performing due diligence, especially as a noob to the world of foreclosure auctions, we recommend you develop relationships with professionals who can advise you. If you're not familiar with the foreclosure laws, housing laws, or landlord-tenant laws in your state, do the work to find a good attorney who is an expert in these specific areas of the law. Don't just go to your neighbor who handles divorces. It could be an expensive mistake. If you're not familiar with the rehab process and you're looking at houses in need of renovation, find and hire a duly licensed, highly qualified general contractor. Check the GC's references. Do your due diligence on the GC first. Then if possible, get them to go to the property with you before the auction. Anyone else you think you might need to work with after the deal, get them involved *before* you place a bid. Tell them about the exact property you're looking at. Ask their opinion. Get their input. Drive by the property with them. Knock on the door. Be bold. Be ballsy.

DO WHAT WE SAY, NOT WHAT WE DO

Honestly, sometimes we think that other people do what we do better. Matt or one of our employees will show up at an auction on a Friday at 11:30, before the auction at noon. That's the first time he actually puts eyes on the property, walks around it, and sees if we have access to the inside of it—and if it's locked, then it's locked (sometimes it's not thoroughly locked). Matt will take pictures while he's on a call with Kev.

Then we meet up with a whole bunch of other investors like ourselves who go to these auctions. We all go from one auction to the next, and see each other at all the different auctions, and they just kind of assume we already know all about this property. They're like, "Oh yeah, nice house. But it sucks that the heating system's been taken." And I'm like, "Oh, it has?" "They're like, "Oh, you didn't know that?" They were already at the house on Wednesday, doing their walk-around and inspecting the property. Sometimes they've knocked on the door and had a conversation with the occupant who lives there. Maybe they've said, "Hey, listen. You know, we're going to buy the place. We're looking to do [whatever]. We could probably work with you if we take over this property. I know a lot of these other investors would just kick you out. So if you wouldn't mind, I'd like to take a look around. If I get to see the inside of it, I'm more likely to take it over, and believe me, you want me taking it over, since I'm going to be nice and flexible unlike one of those other jerks."

These guys are doing their due diligence before the actual auction date. We typically don't for a lot of reasons. One, we're very busy. On average, we're going to dozens of foreclosure auctions every week, so we don't have the time to go beforehand to every single one that comes up. But for folks who aren't attending as many as we are, maybe they're planning to go to one auction and they've marked that date on their calendar. They're out going to the property beforehand. They're talking about it in advance. They're doing a physical evaluation of the property way before the auction date.

That's one of the things we don't really have on our list as part of due diligence is the physical due diligence in advance. But we think you should. And don't just rely on Google Street View, either. Maybe that's helpful to get a sense of the neighborhood, but you might see photos that are two years old. You might not be able to see that the house is rotting. You see a grainy camera shot as the spy car is driving by, but you don't get to see that the paint's all flaking and the siding is rotted. Or that there's a crack in the foundation. And there's an underground oil tank. You don't get to see physical flaws and real red flags. And if you wait until the day of the auction, you might not have the time or presence of mind to notice those things.

We recommend doing your due diligence as far ahead of the auction as possible. Often it takes time, and you won't be able to get enough information last minute to really analyze the deal. The less information you have, the less informed you are, the less chance you have of successfully winning the auction.

If you just look at the property itself, for instance, you're not necessarily going to be able to know what you can or can't do with the property as an investment. You want to know if there are multiple exit strategies. Are there multiple lots? Are there wetlands? Is there any special zoning? If you get that ahead of time, you can make informed decisions. Otherwise, you could go to the property and bid on it as just a regular single-family home. Maybe you'll win, but more likely you'll lose if there are other opportunities that other bidders saw. Knowing all that information could change your bidding strategy; you could actually bid more.

Another problem with waiting until the last minute is that sometimes the sources you need to access will go down. At times the registry of deeds in Massachusetts has gone down. If we're in a time crunch to finish our due diligence, we could be really screwed.

As it stands, many of our deals happen at the very last minute. Often, a lot of the information we need for due diligence isn't available until the last minute. A lot of auctions get canceled at the last minute. A lot of times, information about bid amounts isn't available until the day before the auction, which tends to appeal to the fly-by-the-seat-of-your-pants kind of person. If you're looking to buy a property at a foreclosure auction once every few months, it's easier to stomach. If the stress gets to be too much, you can walk away from any given opportunity because there's another one available next week. But if you're trying to buy five or ten houses a month, then it's going to be an all-the-time grind. For the one-time buyer, it's not that big of a deal. There will be plenty of

BUYER BEWARE

auctions. So if you want to make sure you're going to get the purchase right and you have doubts beforehand for some reason, then don't pull the trigger. Don't bid. Just wait for the next auction. For us, we don't want to miss an opportunity to make $30k here or there because we have payroll and staff and bills and hard money loans that we gotta pay. So we have to be consistently winning these auctions and buying properties, and we don't want to leave money on the table.

So here's a typical due diligence process for us: Remember, we go to dozens of foreclosure auctions for our business every week. Each week, Matt gets a list of the next week's auctions. We also have an assistant who helps with our due diligence research. In each town where a property is located, she calls the tax collector to find out whether there are any taxes owed. Then she calls the municipality and talks to every department including the building department, the health department, the trash department, whatever may exist in that area, to see whether there are any unpaid accounts, to get info about the existence and condition of a septic system, to find out whether the property has ever been condemned, and to learn any info about the size of the house including bedrooms and bathrooms—whatever information they may be able to tell us. Next, she uses the registry of deeds to research all the liens that exist on the property. The registry of deeds will also tell us when any mortgage—including a second mortgage or reverse mortgage—was placed on the property and for how much. That info gives us a clue about how much might have been paid off in the meantime. With all that information, we have enough data to make our go/no-go decision.

The biggest hurdle by far in doing due diligence on properties in foreclosure is that 99% of the time you don't get access inside the property. So how much can you really do? Often the blinds will be down and the windows will be covered. Are the floors buckled? Is there a working heating system? You can call a city collector, call the health department, call the building department. This is all information that's public information. You can get that information. But the actual condition of the property is usually somewhat unknown.

The next big risk factor is figuring out the rehab costs. When you don't have inside access, your knowledge is limited to what you can see. You have to make an educated guess on that. That's where experience comes in. That's also why, if someone's new to this business, having someone come with you who is experienced in renovating properties would be invaluable. They might know about lead paint or asbestos. They may be able to tell you, "In this market, that age of house typically has X issue." Or they'll know whether properties in that section of town are on city sewer or septic, whether the electrical systems often have a problem, or whether all the houses in the neighborhood are historic. They might be able to give you valuable insight: "Just so you know, the historical board in this neighborhood is notoriously difficult to work with."

In most areas, you can find much of that information on public websites with GIS mapping. If the property is located in a historic district, you can talk directly to the historical board and get their regulations. Depending on what you plan to do with the property, your due diligence should include information on the zoning. What is the property zoned for? What are the specific zoning regulations? What's conforming, what's nonconforming?

In truth, there is a lot to know. There's almost no way you can go to your first auction and know absolutely everything there is to know about due diligence. Even after nearly a decade of buying properties in foreclosure, we're still learning.

CHOOSE YOUR OWN ADVENTURE

If you're ready to explore the exciting world of **title research**, *turn to page 154.*

If you're ready for a deep dive into **liens and lien priority**, *turn to page 159.*

If you'd like to take your chances and **skip due diligence**, *turn to page 312.*

TITLE RESEARCH

"Chain of title" is the historical record of ownership transfers for a specific piece of property. Chain of title essentially establishes the legal ownership of real estate, and therefore the owner's right to sell it to someone else. Whenever you buy real estate, one of the critical prepurchase steps is researching title.

BUT IT'S CLEAN!

Another fun fact is that there are multiple types of title other than "clean" title. We recently stumbled into two: "insurable title" and "marketable title." With insurable title, you can close on the property, you can live in it, and you can get homeowner's insurance on it. But the property doesn't have a clean title, so you can't sell it. You have to wait for some period of time—several years—until the title defect expires. Marketable title means it's got a clean title. It's good to resell. There's no waiting period.

We had a property we bought at a foreclosure auction, and right before closing we found out there was a title defect. The closing was delayed while the bank fixed it, but they fixed it. When we closed, our title insurance company wrote a policy for the property. They said," Yep, it's a clean title, a marketable title." All good.

Then we went to wholesale it. For some freaking reason, the buyer's lawyer on the other side kept saying, "No, it's not a clean title. It's not a marketable title. It's only an insurable title. If my client buys it, he can't get title."

And we're like, "That doesn't make sense! What you're referencing was cleaned up. We showed you the documents that prove it was cleaned up! The title insurance company that is going to write title for you says that it's marketable title."

The lawyer put the whole deal at risk based on no real facts. Everyone kept trying to tell him that we had marketable title—our attorney, the title insurance company, even other attorneys we asked. We even went to the CEO of the title company. Even he said, "Yes, it's a hundred percent fine." We had the proof. But what could the buyer do? He needed to follow the advice of his lawyer and rightfully so. But his lawyer was wrong!

It didn't matter. The deal fell through.

JUDICIAL STATES

One thing that's great about foreclosures in judicial states is that when the process gets a judge's approval, it cleans the title. You don't have to worry about title issues because the public was notified of the pending sale. It's been blessed by the court. So in a judicial state, you're guaranteed a clean title. You will still want to review the information about the title that's available online. Some judicial states put everything online. You'll get appraisals, for instance. There will be information on the general condition. You can get a foreclosure worksheet showing other liens, including any federal liens. You'll potentially get much more information on a property in a judicial versus a nonjudicial state.

Compare that with a nonjudicial state, where there's generally just some kind of notice in the classifieds saying, "123 Main Street will have an auction on such and such day. Here's the book and page of it in the registry of deeds. It's a three-bedroom, two-bath house. $5k deposit in certified funds required." Now there's a lot more due diligence you need to do. For that reason, and because that leaves so many more unknowns about the property, we wouldn't bid the same amount on a house in a nonjudicial state as we would for the same house in a judicial state to account for the additional risk.

NONJUDICIAL STATES

In nonjudicial states, title is a significant risk factor. We've won multiple properties where we couldn't close because the property had a bad title, and the bank wasn't willing or able to clean it. The bank had to take the property back as an REO, return our deposit, and then work on cleaning the title before they could sell it. Sometimes the bank does not agree that the title is bad, or sometimes they argue that the sale is "as is, where is" including any issues with the title. That's why you need to research the title before the auction, so that you know what you're taking on if you win the auction. We once bought a two-family in Palmer, Mass, with a title defect that our lawyer found after the auction. The bank argued that there was no title defect. They were like, "Nope, there's not a title defect." Even though there was clearly a title defect, the bank refused to admit it. We weren't comfortable going forward, so we had to walk away from a $10k deposit.

How you go about researching title is different in every state. Depending on the state, you might hire a title company or a lawyer, or you may even be able to perform title research yourself if the state has an online database like in Mass where information is posted online from the registry of deeds. Connecticut has one as well, although it's a little fragmented. If you do the research yourself, you need to know that the database is only as good as the data that's been entered. You know the saying, garbage in, garbage out. So for instance, if the property address is 123 Main Street, you need to search the database for reasonable mistakes that someone might have made when they entered info about the property into the database. You might need to search not just "123 Main Street," but also "123 Main St" and "123 Main St." along with "123 Main Road," "123 Main Drive," and "123 Main Avenue." You also have to check not just the street address, but also the owner's name. Maybe the street wasn't listed when a record was entered into the title database, but it's listed by person.

We recommend hiring an expert, a title company or lawyer, that focuses on title work. If you plan to buy a lot of properties this way, you may want to learn how to do it yourself. After years of paying our lawyer to run title searches for us, we sat down with him for a training on it so we could learn everything we could. We had a rudimentary knowledge of running a search, and we could go on the registry of deeds to get a general idea of the liens tied to a property, but the lawyer's research was much more thorough. So we decided to pay him for a couple of hours of his time so that we could shadow his process and take notes as he ran the search on a property address we gave him.

TITLE INSURANCE

An additional due diligence for these properties is confirming that you can get title insurance. If you win an auction and *then* find out that you can't get title insurance, most auctions are not obligated to return your deposit. But if you can't get title insurance, your attorney might highly recommend that you not close the deal. You could either lose your deposit or end up with a property that doesn't have marketable title—which means you wouldn't be able to sell it for some period of time. In Massachusetts, there's a two-year waiting period to get marketable title. You could really be stuck.

Generally, when someone buys a piece of real estate in a traditional (that is, not foreclosure) transaction, they buy title insurance that protects them from any financial risk that would result from a defect in the title. That's not always possible when buying property in foreclosure. In recent years, some title insurance companies would not issue title policies for occupied foreclosures. Then they would issue policies only for owner-occupied foreclosures. Now they're relaxing those restrictions where we live, but it might (will) be different where you live. And remember: Everything is a negotiation. Since title insurance is an important risk-mitigator, we recommend you pursue it. Find out about how it works on properties in foreclosure in the state where the property is located well before you place a bid.

CHOOSE YOUR OWN ADVENTURE

*If you're ready to roll up your sleeves on researching **liens and lien priority**, turn the page.*

*If all this **due diligence stuff makes your head hurt**, turn to page 314.*

LIENS AND LIEN PRIORITY

The best way to research the existence of liens on a property is through a title search on the registry of deeds. All liens must be recorded on the registry of deeds in order to be valid against the property, so it is *the source* for finding all existing liens. As we've said, we recommend hiring either a title company or an experienced attorney, depending on how searches are usually performed in your state. If you plan to do it yourself, take the time and maybe spend a little money to get a thorough lesson from an expert. Title searches require knowledge and skill, and doing it incorrectly could come back to haunt you.

In addition to the common tax, association, and mortgage liens, you also want to be aware of any federal liens on the property because they work a little differently than other liens. After any foreclosure auction, if the federal government has an income tax lien on the property, then it has the right to take the property either within 120 calendar days from the date of closing on the sale or the state-defined redemption period, whichever is longer. The redemption period varies from state to state, but it's 120 calendar days at a minimum. If it decides to redeem its lien, the federal government could come in, force you to relinquish the property, and pay you only what you actually paid at the auction. So the key is: Do not start any work for 120 calendar days if there is a federal tax lien on the property.

Personally, we have never seen the IRS come back and actually redeem their lien. We've heard that they've almost never done it; 99.999% of the time, the redemption period will pass with no activity. But it's still a risk factor, and to mitigate that risk factor, you just have to wait 120 days. While that may sound easy enough, the carrying costs and delay for an extra four months may make the deal a loser.

Depending on the specific type of lien that is forcing the foreclosure, there may also be other steps you'll want to take in your research.

CHOOSE YOUR OWN ADVENTURE

*If you want to research special considerations related to a **tax foreclosure**, keep reading.*

*If you want to research special considerations related to an **association foreclosure**, turn to page 163.*

*If you want to research special considerations related to a **mortgage foreclosure**, turn to page 165.*

TAX FORECLOSURE

A key point to remember when buying property at a tax foreclosure auction is that the auction will generally wipe out the other liens—mortgage liens, association liens, mechanic's liens, etc. You should confirm that this is true in the specific area where the property is located, but by and large, all local tax liens are super-priority liens that wipe out other liens at auction. The only exception is federal tax liens.

It could also be helpful to know the amount of the lien that's causing the foreclosure, because it may help you assess whether the property is worth pursuing at all. For instance, if the back taxes are $100k and the property isn't worth $50k, you might not even waste your time doing any more due diligence or attending the auction. But if the tax lien is $10k and the property is worth $100k, it could be a good deal.

Assuming the tax lien is a super-priority lien where the property is located, you don't necessarily need to know the amount of the first mortgage. It will get wiped away by the foreclosure process. You don't need to know about any junior liens, either. They also get wiped away.

CHOOSE YOUR OWN ADVENTURE

*If you want to **research a different type of foreclosure**, turn back to page 159.*

*If you're ready to figure out **who's in the house**, turn to page 169.*

ASSOCIATION FORECLOSURE

Whether there are extra steps to your due diligence on an association foreclosure depends on the state. We learned that first-hand, actually. In Massachusetts, condo liens wipe out everything except tax liens. They can be a great way to get a deal for that reason. But in Connecticut, condo associations only have the right to recoup nine months of fees in the foreclosure, and then the foreclosure auction doesn't wipe out the bank's lien. We're all for buying condo liens in Massachusetts, but condo lien foreclosures in Connecticut make very little sense to us— which just shows how much state-to-state differences matter!

We can't speak to the laws in every state, so do your own due diligence on how your state handles condo foreclosures. Typically a state law will govern homeowners' and condo associations, and detail how association liens are handled. Usually there is also information on a state website; you just have to know how to search for it. Sometimes the laws are very legalese and hard to understand for a layperson. If you plan to bid on an association foreclosure, talk to a lawyer who is knowledgeable about foreclosures first, and don't be afraid to ask, "What does this law actually mean? How does this process play out in the real world?"

CHOOSE YOUR OWN ADVENTURE

*If you want to **research a different type of foreclosure**, turn back to page 159.*

*If you're ready to figure out **who's in the house**, turn to page 169.*

MORTGAGE FORECLOSURE

One of the biggest pitfalls with properties in bank foreclosure is the existence of higher-priority municipal liens, primarily tax liens. It can be a costly mistake to buy a property in a mortgage foreclosure only to discover afterward that there's also a municipal lien on it. If you don't know how to research tax liens, hire a lawyer to do a title rundown for you so that you can have a better idea of all the liens that exist—like that $20k outstanding tax lien on the cute one-bedroom single-family you've got your eye on.

It's equally important to know which mortgage is causing the foreclosure. You might assume it's the first mortgage—but that could be a dangerous assumption. Have your real estate lawyer confirm that it's the first mortgage. Remember that a second-mortgage foreclosure does not wipe out a first mortgage. Know your lien priority.

THAT'S GOTTA HURT

We once won a fully renovated property at a first-mortgage foreclosure auction in Connecticut, which had previously been purchased at a second-mortgage foreclosure by a contractor who immediately started working on the rehab. The second lienholder had held a foreclosure auction for $90k. The guy bid $200k and won—but it was a second lien. The first lien was around $45k. The winner thought he didn't have to worry about the first lien because his lawyer told him that the excess between his winning bid of $200k and the second lien of $45k would trickle up to pay off the first lien. But that's not how it works. Any excess money from the winning bid is trickle-down, not trickle-up. Based on bad advice from his lawyer and believing that he'd bought it free and clear, he renovated the property.

Then the first lienholder finally foreclosed. For some reason they took longer to foreclose than the second lienholder had taken. We don't know if the title was defective or what the issue was. But five or six months later, Kev shows up at the first-mortgage foreclosure auction and sees people renovating the house. They're painting and installing flooring at that point. They're literally done with the renovation and finishing up the new windows, siding, roof. It's a fully renovated property.

Kev finds the contractor and asks him if he's worried about the first-mortgage foreclosure about to take place. The guy doesn't care. He's like, "Oh, I'm good." He has no idea that he's about to lose the house. The auction starts with an opening bid of $45k. Knowing the value is probably about $400k, we bid up to $250k. And we win. Now we're working on the closing process through the court, which always takes a bit longer in a judicial state.

We later found out that the guy who bought it in the second-lien foreclosure took out a hard money loan for the purchase and renovation. The hard money lender also didn't do their due diligence. They didn't realize it was a second-mortgage foreclosure. Since we bid $250k for the first mortgage, any excess after any property taxes and the first mortgage lien are paid off will trickle down to the guy who bought the property at the second-mortgage auction. So he will basically recoup—well, the hard money lender will recoup—most of their costs. We think they'll still be out a little because he may have $300k in it all told. He'll have to pay the deficiency to the hard money lender, or else the hard money lender will go after him.

The guy was screwed by his own ignorance. He should never have gotten a hard money loan or started the rehab on a second-mortgage foreclosure. He should have understood the chain of title and gotten a lawyer who actually knows what they're doing. One lawyer is not the same as another. Just because somebody's an attorney doesn't mean they're a real estate attorney.

The registry of deeds will show you the issue date, type, and amount of all the mortgage and other liens on the property, including bank liens and junior liens. Often the registry will show the note with all the terms, including whether it's a regular or reverse mortgage.

Keep in mind that when the foreclosure is based on a mortgage lien, you won't know the amount of the total lien unless you can get in touch with the bank. That's because they don't have to disclose all the fees included in the lien, such as late fees and legal fees. You're bidding kind of blind, and you have to make an educated guess about the extra costs.

REVERSE MORTGAGES

Reverse mortgage foreclosures are more rare, but they happen when an owner dies and no one takes over the estate. If the foreclosure is the result of a first mortgage that's a reverse mortgage, the foreclosure might be a goldmine. With a regular mortgage, the bank gives you a lump sum up front to buy the house and you then pay the loan back in small increments over time, usually fifteen to thirty years. With a reverse mortgage, the process happens in reverse. The bank establishes the total loan amount and then pays it out in monthly increments over time, typically thirty years, with the idea that the debt will be repaid in the future, usually from the sale of the house.

With information from the registry of deeds on the loan amount, origination date, and interest rate, you can estimate the amount of the outstanding lien. If the loan was made four years ago for $250k at 4%, you can figure that the bank has paid out a little over $20k. Maybe they've thrown in some additional fees, but you can guess that the foreclosure amount is no more than $30k. So you can figure that the bank is going to auction the property for $30k when the house is worth close to $300k. That's a massive spread. So you know that's a killer auction to attend.

Now, if it's a 29-year-old reverse mortgage, well, it's probably not worth going to.

CHOOSE YOUR OWN ADVENTURE

*If you want to **research a different type of foreclosure**, turn back to page 159.*

*If you're ready to figure out **who's in the house**, keep reading.*

WHO'S IN THE HOUSE

Dealing with occupants is not for the faint of heart. It can lead to very expensive mistakes. From our experience, occupants of the properties we've bought represent the biggest risk in the foreclosure-buying process because people are unpredictable and, well, they're *people.* The law wants to protect people, so there are always a lot of laws about what the new property owner can and cannot do when dealing with occupants.

Keep in mind that it's also the easiest risk to mitigate: just don't buy occupied property. Now you're dealing with only the physical, tangible stuff. "I can see that the heat doesn't work. I can see that the plumbing doesn't work. This hole needs to be fixed." You can understand that risk. You can virtually guarantee that you're not going to have an occupant problem if the place has no occupant.

If the property is occupied, go a few days early to see if you can talk to the occupant and get them to let you take a look around. Dangle a carrot to do so. In addition to giving you an information advantage about the condition of the property, it can also help you estimate how much it might cost to deal with the occupant, and whether they're open to moving or likely to dig in.

We've said it before: You can have a tremendous advantage if you are willing and able to buy an occupied property. A lot of bidders back out when they realize there's a person living in the house. In fact, it's such a turn-off for most buyers that a guy in our area got in trouble for staging vacant houses as if they were occupied. He'd get the power turned on so that he could turn on the lights and make it look lived in. If it was winter, he'd even plow the driveway. He got found out and was arrested and fined—so we don't recommend this as a strategy.

If you can succeed at buying a property that other people will avoid, you'll get a way better deal because there's less competition. We've legit had people leave an auction when they saw an occupant in the house. And yet we've gotten people out of houses within thirty days for $750 and the cost of a moving van. Then we turned around and sold the same house within sixty days for a profit of $100k. So if you are willing to roll the dice a little bit and able to hedge your bet enough to where you can make a deal work, it can be tremendously advantageous to you financially.

One thing you can do to hedge your bet is evaluate the people at the property. Knock on the door and attempt a conversation. If you do that, and then socially engineer a way to get in with that person, that's completely okay. If the occupant allows you access to the home, that gives you a massive advantage. That's a technique people really do use. We don't do it as much, but other bidders absolutely do. If the auction is scheduled for Friday, they'll go there on a Tuesday, they'll knock, they'll catch somebody at home, and they'll say, "Hey, listen, I know this place is up for auction. If somebody else buys it, they're just going to throw you out as fast as they can. They're going to serve you with eviction paperwork. I'm looking to buy it, and if I were to bid, you should hope I get it because I'll be happy to work with you. Maybe we can cut a deal. But the only way I'd be able to buy it is if I know a little bit more about this property. So would you have a minute? Could I take a look around at this property so that hopefully I'm the one who buys it?" Make a case that there's something good in it for the occupant, and that's why the occupant should let you have access.

So knock on the door. Take several steps back so that you're not in their face. Step down off the front steps so you're at a lower position. Use your high-pitched voice. "Hi there, my name's [insert name here]. You don't know me. And I know this might be kind of weird, but this place is up for auction on Friday. I'm planning on attending and looking to buy the place. I see that it's occupied. I didn't know somebody was living here. Did you know it was up for auction?"

Maybe they're a bona fide tenant, which is a tenant with an arm's length agreement who pays reasonable consideration (not the daughter of the owner who pays $20 a month). Maybe they've been renting this house from the guy who's not paying his mortgage. Maybe they're like, "What are you talking about? Oh my God! I gotta call my landlord. I've been paying him rent this whole time. Are you going to kick me out?"

You could say, "Well, listen, no, no, no. Wow. I'm really glad I connected with you because I actually buy properties like this quite a bit. I know a lot of the other guys who do this, and I want to work with the people living in these properties. All these other guys, they'll just throw you out. They're all bad. You don't want them to buy this place. I'm a good guy and I'm going to work with you. But you know what? To ensure that I have the ability to buy this place, it'd be really helpful if I could see the inside and see what I'm looking to buy. That way, I can make sure I can outbid everybody else. Do you have a minute? Do you think maybe I could take a quick peek inside, see if the heating system's up to date, that kind of thing?"

Your main goal in this conversation is to get information about the property and to get permission to look around. Your second goal is to begin establishing the expectation that you'll want the house vacant if you become the owner, and that you can achieve that in a lot of different ways. You might let the occupant know, "The auction is next week. Then if I win, it'll be several weeks until I become the owner of record. So at this point, we're talking another month before I'd be looking to have the place vacant. It's not like it has to happen tomorrow."

A conversation like that could start easing them into the idea that it's time to leave without panicking them. If you just say, "Hey, I want the house empty," people's minds start scrambling: "I don't know where I'm gonna go! I don't have a place! I need time. Oh my God, I need money! I need to find a place!" You're trying to prevent that by saying, "It's not gonna happen overnight, but I am gonna want the house to be empty if I'm the new owner. My plan for this is to move in with my family" or "to fix it up" or "to sell it," whatever the case may be, "and obviously I need it vacant for that. It won't happen overnight, but do you already have a plan now that you know this is coming? Do you have any idea where you're gonna be going? How long is it gonna take? Here's my number. If you move out before I become the owner, please drop me a line. Otherwise, if I win the auction and haven't heard from you, I'm sure we'll talk again."

Try to get the occupant warmed up to the idea that they will soon have to vacate. It's just a matter of exactly when, once you become the owner. You're setting the stage for a subsequent conversation after you win the auction that goes something like, "Hi, we talked a month ago. I just wanted to follow up. What is your plan?"

At that point if they answer, "Well, I need time! I need to find a place," you can respond with, "You've already had a month. When you say 'time,' do you mean a couple more days? Because you've already had a whole month since we talked." It will be harder for them to squirm and claim they had no idea any of this was coming.

Our experience is that often people don't act until they have no choice. If you give them six months to make a plan, they still won't have one at the end of six months. They don't do crap until the night before the deadline, like Kev studying for a test.

But now at least you've talked your way in, and you've also gotten some idea of the occupant's state of mind. Hopefully you've cut the adversarial tension between you. Maybe you're even on the same side, working through a common problem: You both need to figure out the best way to vacate this house after the auction.

CHOOSE YOUR OWN ADVENTURE

*If you're ready to go by the property and **check it out**, turn the page.*

*If all this **due diligence stuff seems overblown**, turn to page 313.*

CHECK IT OUT

A bidder who has the ability to get inside when others can't will have an information advantage when calculating how much they can pay. That's because once you're inside, you can do a much more thorough job of checking the physical condition and accurately estimating rehab costs. You can look for evidence of deferred maintenance, vandalism, or even illegal activity—all of which will help you calculate how much it's going to cost to make the property ready for use.

A lot of vacant properties have had neighbor kids running in and out of them for years. If a thirteen-year-old can go inside to play, there's no reason an investor can't poke their head into a poorly secured door or window. We're not condoning breaking and entering. We're just saying use your judgment. It's very advantageous for a lot of reasons to know what's going on inside the property.

But because getting access inside is generally impossible before the auction, we recommend several other steps you can take to assess a property. First off, call the city or county health department to find out whether it has a septic system and, if so, when it was installed and last inspected. Septic systems can be expensive to repair, and hard to inspect because they're underground. If you don't do your due diligence ahead of the auction, you could be looking at a $50k job for a whole new leach field and holding tank.

It's also good to be aware of the specific issues that are common where you live, which is where it can be valuable to have an experienced GC on speed dial. In our area, for instance, a lot of homes are older. If a home was built before 1978, the state assumes that it's had lead paint in it at one point or another—and there is a law about remediating lead paint. If you intend to rent out the property, you need to get an inspection letter for which you pay a lot of money that says the home is "lead-safe" for kids under six. That doesn't mean there's no lead; it just means that the home is in compliance with the law. Because the process is expensive, a lot of rental properties have never been inspected. But not having a lead certificate for a rental property can expose a landlord to potential liability. That's why we check the state's lead database to see whether a property has already been inspected. If we're interested in a home built before 1978, we assume we'll have to remediate the lead if we search the database and find no current reports. Then we figure the cost of remediation into our rehab plan and bid strategy.

Connecticut doesn't have these laws though, so we don't have to include those costs in our rehab estimates for properties we buy in that state. That's why you need to know about all the laws that apply to health and safety in the area where the property is located. They can impact the requirements and the cost of a rehab.

CHOOSE YOUR OWN ADVENTURE

*If you're **still interested in the property** after checking it out, turn the page.*

*If you **haven't been able to get any access to the property** at all, turn to page 305.*

LOCATION, LOCATION, LOCATION

Often you can get access to an online GIS map to see the boundary lines, zoning, wetlands, and other relevant features of a property. This information can be very helpful so you know what other ways there may be to use the property.

Several other aspects of location are worth paying attention to in your due diligence as well, in terms of both the value of the property and its suitability for your game plan. Especially if you're a homeowner, location will matter a lot. If you're going to buy the property to live in it, you might be looking to live in a specific city. It has to be near where you work or in your kid's school system. But if you're buying it as an investment property, you probably don't care that much, as long as it's not too, too far away from your target area.

That said, areas that might not be attractive to you as a homeowner could be very appealing to you as an investor. If you can get a property for $30k, put in $10k to rehab it, and then rent it for $1,500 a month, you're making great cash flow. So whether a location is suitable really depends on your exit strategy for the property.

Another consideration in terms of location is whether the property fits your strategy given your own location. For instance, if it needs a lot of rehab, do you have a team set up in the area where the property is located and the ability to manage that team? We learned that lesson from the house we bought in Wilton, Connecticut. Even after that experience of losing money, we'd still buy a property there again if the conditions were right. The deal could work if the property needed very little rehab, for instance, or if we could acquire it at a big enough discount and we had a local crew already lined up to do the work. In other words, there's almost no location we *wouldn't* consider. We'd just be very, very sure beforehand that every detail of the property and the location worked for our strategy and our business model.

Obviously, the neighborhood impacts what people are willing to pay for the property, either to buy or to rent. What kind of market is it? Is it a C-class or D-class neighborhood, or is it more of a premium area? If you're planning to use the property as a rental, the answer will impact the cash flow you can assume. Not only will rents be lower in a D-class neighborhood compared with a B-class neighborhood, but also maintenance expenses are likely to be much higher. The vacancy rate and nonpayment rates will also be higher in more challenging areas. Our business has survived because we came up with a process for effectively managing sub-prime properties located in places that other investors might find less desirable. As a general rule for buying investment property, we recommend paying less to acquire a property that will produce less income and/or carry higher ongoing expenses.

UNDERSTAND THE MARKET

Location is obviously an important factor when it comes time to run a comparative market analysis (CMA) and calculate the property's ARV. When you're doing your due diligence, make note of any special features that could impact the value, positively or negatively. For example, where we live, as in many areas of the country, proximity to water has a big impact on value. If the property has a view of water, that tends to boost the value. If it's directly on the water, the value could increase by double or even more. Features like this vary from area to area; maybe in your area the money shot is a view of the mountains or access to public land.

It's helpful for that reason to really understand the area before you buy so that you can assess how marketable the property will be. That means understanding what sells and what doesn't in the area. Maybe ranch-style homes and contemporaries are popular in the neighborhood, while log cabins are out of favor. Meanwhile, if the very same log cabin were located in the mountains, it would command a very high value.

In our area, ranches generally bring high value because they're so simple. A lot of people like one-story homes, while two-story and split-level homes are harder to sell. Contemporary homes appeal to a slice of the market, while cottage-style homes and colonials tend to attract a broader segment of buyers. Once again, here's where it can be very helpful to have an experienced local realtor on your team who can run CMAs and give you insights to guide your purchase and your subsequent plan for the property.

PLAY ZONE DEFENSE

Understanding the zoning of a property is an important and sometimes overlooked part of due diligence. Sure, you might *think* the property is a two-family based on how it's being used, only to find out that it's actually only zoned as a single-family. You're doing your calculations on the assumption that it's a two-family, and then you close on it and the building inspector's like "No, this is only zoned for single. You can't get a variance." That changes the cash flow assumption on the property, so it changes your ARV. It changes *everything*.

Another consideration is whether the property is in an area with limitations or rules about what you can do when you rehab, such as a historic district or homeowners' association. If the association bylaws dictate your options, it could change how you handle your rehab or even whether you can use the property as you intend. Understanding all that before you buy is important.

We were once interested in a property in a historic district, and it needed repairs to the exterior. When we researched the district's rules, we learned we couldn't just swap out the old shingle siding for new because the existing shingles on the property had been out of production for fifty years. We'd have to go before the historic review board for permission to use whatever we selected as a replacement. The railing system on the front porch also wasn't up to code, but we wouldn't be able to just bring it up to code without a lot of time and expense dealing with the unique architecture of the building. All of those considerations would have impacted our rehab costs, our holding period, potentially our plan for the property—basically every aspect of the deal. That's why we generally stay away from properties that are zoned historic.

If we know that a property has unique zoning and we decide to pursue it anyway, then we factor in the additional cost—but we've seen people get really surprised. We've also seen owners try to get around the rules only to pay for it later when a neighbor reports them for doing work that's not approved and they get it hit with a stop work order.

Now, it's time to decide your next move.

CHOOSE YOUR OWN ADVENTURE

*If you finished all the due diligence on the location and the **property works for your game plan**, turn to page 183.*

*If you finished all the due diligence on the location and the **property doesn't suit your game plan**, turn to page 305.*

FORECLOSURE DUE DILIGENCE CHECKLIST

- **Understand the Foreclosure Process:** Understand how foreclosures work in the area the property is located:

  - Is it in a judicial state, a nonjudicial state, or a state with a hybrid approach?

  - What amount of deposit is required?

  - Where will the auction be hosted?

- **Review the Title:** It is essential to understand which lien on the property is foreclosing and where they stand in order of the title. Many local governments now put their registry of deeds online for ease of access. The registry of deeds may also include copies of property surveys.

- **Call the City Tax Collector:** Since municipal liens are the priority liens above all others, you want to know whether any of the following liens exist on the property: water, sewer, electric, gas, taxes, trash, and any other assessments or fees charged by the local government with jurisdiction over the property.

- **Call the City Building and Health Department:** Talk to these departments. They will often have invaluable information about the property including permits pulled, septic information, code violations, condemnation, etc.

- **Check with the IRS for Liens**: Find out if the property has an IRS lien against it by calling the IRS. Federal liens are public information, so anyone is entitled to know whether a lien exists on a property. If it does, be aware that there is a 120-day redemption period after the foreclosure sale, during which time the former homeowner could pay off the lien and retain the property.

- **Check the GIS and Zoning Maps:** Often you can get access to an online GIS map to see the boundary lines, zoning, wetlands, and other relevant features of the property. This information can be very helpful so you know what other ways there may be to use the property.

- **Check Recent Sales Activity:** Learn to evaluate like-kind sales so that you can determine what the estimated ARV will be, after your value-adds like renovation, repairs, and rehab. If you can access the MLS, it's a great resource for finding the value of comparable properties ("comps") in terms of similar age, style, square footage, number of bedrooms, presence (or not) of a garage, existence (or not) of a basement, and whether the homes in the area have been rehabbed recently. In some states, you can see what properties recently sold on websites like Zillow, Trulia, Redfin, and Realtor.com. If you don't have access to any of that info, talk to a knowledgeable local real estate agent or appraiser who can run a comp report for you.

- **Check Out the Neighborhood:** It's important to understand what is going on in the neighborhood that could impact the value of the property. Is it quiet? Is it busy? Is it on a main drag or in a *cul-de-sac*? Is it in a historic district? What are the neighbors like? What's the general condition of other properties on the street?

- **Inspect the Property:** This can be one of the hardest parts because most of the time you will not have inside access. It is hard to know what you don't know. Our recommendations are to always err on the side of caution when guesstimating the condition of the property. Also, can you tell whether it's vacant or occupied?

- **Talk to the Occupants:** If the property is occupied, go a few days early to see if you can talk to the occupants and get them to let you take a look around. In addition to giving you an information advantage about the condition of the property, it can also help you assess whether the occupant is open to moving or likely to dig in, and how much it might cost to deal with them.

CHAPTER 7

STICK TO YOUR NUMBERS

Once you've done your due diligence and confirmed that the property could work for you, it's time to calculate your Maximum Allowable Offer (MAO). This number is the most you can bid for the property, no matter what happens once you get to the auction. Your MAO is based on several factors, including your specific game plan and everything that you've learned from due diligence about the work you'll have to do on the property to make it meet your needs.

The MAO is also based on your own tolerance for risk, meaning how close to the margin are you willing to play. If you're a noob, we recommend you be conservative in your risk appetite. If you've never bought a property at a foreclosure auction before, set yourself up for success this first time. Remember: The best deal may be the one you walk away from.

We like to try to work on our MAO a little ahead of time. Sometimes we wait until the last minute, but ideally we'll do it over the weekend before the auction. The information we have to pull together for the calculation includes:

TWO GUYS TAKE ON THE MAXIMUM ALLOWABLE OFFER (MAO)

Formula: MAO = [ARV/(1+TargetROI)] - (Closing Costs + Holding Costs + Rehab Costs + Other Costs)

Where:

ARV: *Based on comps in the area, the estimated after repair value of the home after all planned repairs are completed.*

Target ROI: *The target return on investment or profit you and your investors want to make given the risks of the transaction and the market fundamentals.*

Closing Costs: *Fees and costs to complete the initial purchase transaction and, if the plan is to resell it, the subsequent sale of the property.*

Holding Costs: *All recurring costs associated with owning the property, excluding rehab costs and one-time expenses. Holding costs typically include the cost of financing as well as utilities, insurance, property taxes, and association dues and levies.*

Rehab Costs: *The estimated expense to renovate the property in order to make it usable for its intended purpose, whether to buy-and-hold or flip.*

Other Costs: *All other one-time costs necessary to execute the investment strategy, including curing other outstanding liens or title issues, dealing with occupants, and paying commissions to real estate agents for selling a renovated property.*

Example:

ARV: *Let's say we found a house that we estimate will have an ARV of $200k after we complete the renovation. That's our starting point.*

Target ROI: *At one time we used 50% as our target ROI, and we were still able to win a lot of foreclosure auctions. But as the market heated up in recent years, we've had to take slimmer margins in order to be competitive against other bidders—some of whom were willing to take 10% margins. Unless we're wholesaling the property, a margin that slim is just too risky for us given all the unknowns with these properties, so we stick with 40%.*

Closing Costs: *Let's assume that we plan to fix and flip this property, so we expect one closing on the purchase post-auction and another closing when we sell it. Our typical cost per closing is about $2,500, so we estimate $5k for two closings.*

Holding Costs: *Often one of our biggest holding costs is the cost of borrowing the money to finance the purchase. Let's say we're using hard money at 10% annual interest based on the ARV. Since we expect our holding period to be six months, we'll budget $5k for interest expense. Then we'll budget another $5k for utilities, insurance, and property taxes, bringing our total estimated holding costs to $10k.*

Rehab Costs: *Obviously rehab costs vary widely from property to property, but for the sake of an easy example, let's just say we estimate another $15k for a light rehab.*

Other Costs: *We always call the municipality where the property is located to confirm the amount of all outstanding liens so that we can include the cost of paying them off in our calculations. This step is where a lot of deals fall apart, so it's a critically important step. Since we plan to flip the property retail, we'll pay our real estate agent a commission on the sale. And finally we typically budget $5k for dealing with occupants if we know someone is* *living in the house. Let's say there's another $15k in other costs between the liens, commissions, and occupants.*

Now we have all the data to calculate our MAO:

MAO	=	**[ARV / (1 + Target Profit Margin)] -** *(Closing Costs + Holding Costs + Rehab Costs + Other Costs)*
	=	*[$200k / (1 + 40%)] - ($5k + $10k + $15k + $15k)*
	=	*[$200k / (1 + 0.4)] - ($45k)*
	=	*[$200k / 1.4] - $45k*
	=	*$143k - $45k*
	=	*$98k*

Now we have our MAO of $98k. That is the maximum we can pay for the property when we get to the auction, no matter what happens once the bidding starts. The only way we could pay more would be to do more due diligence before the auction to 1) find hidden value to increase the ARV, or 2) reduce one of our costs. Otherwise, we stick to this number.

If we win, we'll pay $98k for the acquisition, and we'll have a budget of $45k for the other costs of fixing and flipping the property. If we later sell it for at least the $200k ARV that we expect, we'll make a return of $57k, or 40% on our total investment of $143k:

ROI $ = $200k sale price - $143k total investment = $57k

ROI % = $57k profit / $143k total investment = 40%

TAKE A STRESS TEST

When the market is unpredictable, it is not a time to get too risky. It is a time to be a little bit more conservative. What makes a market unpredictable? High inflation, for one. Changing interest rates, for another. When we see these indicators in the real estate market, we take an extra step to vet our deals—and we recommend that you do too.

After you've come up with your cash flow estimates based on your assumptions for how you'll use the property, run a "stress test" to see how far you can bend your assumptions before they break. Fast forward down the road a few steps into your strategy: What amount do you think the property is going to refi for when it comes time to pull money out, and what happens if it refi's for less? How much money do you plan to pull out, and what happens to your financial plan if you can only get 80% of that amount? You have to take some educated guesses in terms of what the property value will be when it comes time to refinance and what a bank's going to lend you.

Let's say the bank will refinance at 70% of the value of the property, and you estimate the value will be $300k after the rehab. Is 70% of $300k enough to pay back your hard money loan, put your investment money back into your pocket, or even put extra cash in your pocket so that you have money to buy your next property? What if the bank changes its lending policy to 80% LTV? You have to figure out the answers to those questions early on in the process, which can be challenging when the real estate market is changing rapidly. When things are uncertain, that means you have to act more conservatively and you have to know what your risk tolerance is.

We stress test our deals the same way. Whether we're going to auction or we're buying a property another way, for instance, we know we're unlikely to close in sixty days. So we run our numbers with an extra hundred basis points, which is an additional 1%, in the cost of our capital to stress test the deal. If today's interest rate is 6%, we run the numbers assuming the interest rate is 7%. Then we adjust the assumptions. If we have to put more money down, for example, then what does the deal look like? Does it still work for us?

Run your numbers with the worst-case scenario that you think could happen. If you're still comfortable with the deal, then move forward. Once you've done that, maybe rates don't go up as high as you thought so you end up doing even better than you estimated.

GO DEEP

As you're coming up with your own MAO, get comfortable with all the underlying assumptions and definitions in the formula. Run a few hypothetical calculations, which will help you understand how changing one of the assumptions impacts the amount you can pay for a property and still hit your target.

CHOOSE YOUR OWN ADVENTURE

*If you're interested in our approach to calculating the **after repair value** along with one way we've found to gain a competitive advantage, turn the page.*

*If you want to learn more about **closing costs**, turn to page 194.*

*If you'd like to read more about calculating **holding costs**, turn to page 195.*

*If you'd like to know how Matt comes up with his estimates for **rehab costs**, turn to page 197.*

*To read more about **other costs**, turn to page 203.*

*To learn more about how the **profit margin** impacts the MAO and your likelihood of winning the auction, turn to page 205.*

*If you're ready to **head to the auction**, turn to page 207.*

AFTER REPAIR VALUE

The first step in calculating the maximum allowable offer is coming up with the ARV, the after repair value. Knowing the ARV is the starting point for the calculation of your maximum bid. It's the end value from which you back out the rest of your numbers (like the purchase price, the rehab costs, and your profit). You're estimating the value of a fully rehabbed house and making adjustments for what your house will have that others in the neighborhood don't, and features other houses have that yours won't.

We used to rely on Zillow estimates for our ARV, but we haven't for years now because Zillow's estimates take several months to catch up to the market. Especially in a volatile market where prices change quickly, you really need to look at what is selling in the market currently. When the market was going crazy in 2020 and 2021, we had buyers tell us, "the Zillow estimate says this" when they submitted their offers. Then we'd have an appraiser give us an estimate of the value based on recent comps, and it was often tens of thousands of dollars higher than what Zillow said. You can look at Zillow for recent sales, but the best source is really the realtors' Multiple Listing Service (MLS).

Here's where your network comes in again. If you have a friend who's a realtor, they can help find the actual recent comps in the last six months within a half-mile radius. In certain areas you might go a little farther out for comps, to help you make sure you capture as much value as possible. Looking at the MLS will give you a much more real-time view of what's happening in the area, so that you don't end up trying to catch a falling knife in a downmarket or shortchange your profit in an upmarket.

If you don't know much about the area where the house is located, leverage technology as much as possible. Look at all the real estate sites to see what the houses are like in that area. Use Google Street View to check out the neighborhood. The same advice applies to understanding the fit and finish your property will need in order to be competitive. Here's when you can use sites like Zillow and Realtor.com to see how other houses on the market right now are finished. If you have access to the MLS, you can look at the properties that sold quickly to see how they were finished. You'll be able to see from the pictures whether all the updated houses in the area have granite, designer backsplashes, and wood floors—or not—so that you can plan your renovation while being mindful not to over-renovate.

If you anticipate using the property as a rental, you can use an online rent calculator geared to landlords to get an idea of what it would rent for.

HOW TO GET A COMPETITIVE ADVANTAGE

Whenever we go to these auctions, we know that a potential homeowner can always pay more than we can. If a potential homeowner is there, we know we're getting outbid if they're at all savvy—*unless* we can find a value-add that they can't see. Having bought a lot of properties over the past decade, we can now see value-adds where others don't. If you pay attention to potential value-adds, you can increase your ARV to include the additional value. The increased ARV will result in a higher MAO, giving you a competitive advantage.

For instance, often we can find buildable lots that a homeowner doesn't see. If the house is on a double lot, for instance, we may be able to sell off the lot, making an additional $70k. That increases the ARV we include in our MAO calculation by $70k. Meanwhile, the potential homeowner is thinking, "Ooh, it's got a big yard."

Or maybe we notice that the lot has a hundred feet of road frontage, which means we could subdivide it. We know that it costs $2k to subdivide a lot, and lots in our area go for $70k, so there's a $68k profit to be made. Now we can add that to our ARV and calculate our bid with the additional profit built in. Now all of a sudden, we can bid more than the homeowner. We've definitely gotten $30k and even $40k more value out of a property because we knew the zoning law, and then we were able to bid higher and win the auction.

That said, do not include in your bid the value of any exceptional personal property you see on the property. Consider it gravy because you don't know what's going to happen to it before you close. We were once outbid at a foreclosure auction in Long Meadow. We thought the guy who won overpaid by a lot. When he finally got inside the property, he found a safe left behind by the prior owner. He hired a safecracker to open it, and they found jewels inside that he subsequently got appraised and then sold for over $100k. But he didn't know that when he placed his bid! That was just an incredibly lucky break.

If the foreclosure happened because the owner passed away, maybe an heir comes back. Even though the chances of people coming back are slim, they still have the right to go into the property and grab any personal belongings. You don't know what they could still take because the deed hasn't been transferred to you yet. So until you have the deed in your name, don't count on taking possession of any items that could be easily removed. Someone could walk away with jewels and even cars. Someone could break in. We've seen it happen: Maybe there are multiple bidders at the auction. You win, but they saw the same value that you saw in the personal items. While you're waiting to close, they break in and steal all of it. It wouldn't be the first time that's happened.

So consider that stuff gravy, even if it's rich gravy.

CHOOSE YOUR OWN ADVENTURE

*If you want to **understand other variables in the MAO calculation**, turn back to page 183.*

*If you're ready to **head to the auction**, turn to page 207.*

CLOSING COSTS

Closing costs are the upfront fees you pay when you sign the deal to purchase the property from a foreclosure auction, including title insurance, attorney fees, and any points on the loan that finances the purchase. Like so many aspects of these deals, closing costs for foreclosures will vary from state to state. A lot of people use 4% of the total purchase price as an estimate, comparable with a nonforeclosure real estate purchase. If you're using a hard money loan, which will typically carry higher points, then you may want to estimate closing costs at 5% or 6% just to be safe.

CHOOSE YOUR OWN ADVENTURE

If you want to **understand other variables in the MAO calculation***, turn back to page 183.*

If you're ready to **head to the auction***, turn to page 207.*

HOLDING COSTS

Managing your holding costs can be the difference between a win and a loss. Holding costs will vary from transaction to transaction based on a number of factors, including especially your game plan for the property; whether the property is vacant or occupied and, if so, how quickly you're able to deal with the occupants; how well you manage the rehab if that's part of your strategy; and obviously simply the cost of the property: A more expensive property will necessarily come with higher holding costs.

If you're planning to fix-and-flip and the property is occupied, the length of time it will take to get the property vacant so that you can take the next steps will depend a lot on the landlord-tenant laws in your state. In Massachusetts we typically allow three to four months just to get an occupant out.

Once the house is vacant, the time it takes to complete a rehab depends on the scope of work. It could take anywhere from two weeks to six months or more. While the costs of the rehab are not part of holding costs, the carrying costs of the property while the rehab happens are— so you want to manage the rehab in a way that minimizes your holding costs. This is where your professional network comes in again: The better your contractors are at estimating their level of effort on projects, the more accurate your estimate of holding costs can be.

MIND THE EXIT

Matt won his personal house at a foreclosure auction and borrowed hard money not only for the acquisition, but also for the renovation. He's got our business to run, so when he bought the house for himself, he tried not to make it too much of a priority that would take away from our business. As a result, the renovation took two years. The refinancing process was part of the holdup, but he ended up paying a lot more in holding costs than he originally estimated because the exit dragged on and on.

While the exit in this case was refinancing into a conventional mortgage, the exit can be any one of several strategies. It could be reselling the property or refinancing to pull out equity for a subsequent investment, for instance. Whatever your exit strategy is, you've got to keep it in sight to keep your holding costs in check.

CHOOSE YOUR OWN ADVENTURE

*If you want to **understand other variables in the MAO calculation**, turn back to page 183.*

*If you're ready to **head to the auction**, turn to page 207.*

REHAB COSTS

Obviously, we have to run our estimates using costs of materials and labor at the time of the estimate. We can't predict the future, and that fact presents a serious challenge when inflation is high. It's been a real problem for us in the past couple of years as the prices of building materials skyrocketed. By the time we closed on some of our acquisitions, we had to throw our rehab estimates out the window because we were seeing 50%-60% price increases in materials, not to mention the cost of labor going through the roof. Our rehab budgets were not even in the realm of possibility. Luckily, we've now seen both materials and labor costs trickle down a little bit, but we've also had a hard time just finding labor to get our projects done—which can impact our holding costs.

That's just one example of why we recommend you overestimate your rehab costs. The other is that there are so many unknowns with property you buy at a foreclosure auction. That's why it's also important to try to look at the property. If someone's living in it, knock on the door and try to talk your way inside. If you can do that, you'll have a leg up on any other bidders who don't get that access.

ASSESS THE PROPERTY (AS BEST YOU CAN)

When we're ready to calculate the rehab costs, we'll go to the property and inspect as much of it as we can. We'll take pictures and share them with our partners in a group thread, and together we come up with a repair estimate and contingency based on all the risks we identify. You want to take the time to walk through as much of the property as possible and look closely at everything: the roof, the heating system, the siding, the windows.

When Matt can't get inside a property to run his estimates, he takes a top-down approach based on what he can see from the outside, starting with the roof and working his way down to the foundation. Then he makes assumptions about the interior. We recommend using a drone to inspect the chimney, roof, and other exterior features you can't see from the ground. First, he looks at the condition of the roof from every possible angle, followed by the chimney. He's looking to see whether it needs repointing and whether there is a chimney cap. Then he looks at the siding, determining whether it's dated in either condition or style and what it's made of to figure out whether it will need to be repaired or replaced. If any of it is missing and the wood underneath has been opened and exposed, there might be rot. Also look at the gutters, which are generally not that expensive to replace.

Next, he looks at the age and condition of the windows. If they're old, we usually replace them with newer, more energy-efficient ones. Then he looks at the decks and porches, particularly the condition of the floorboards and the spindles on the railings as well as the stain or paint. We're looking for ways we might be able to save on costs by saving boards that are in good condition. Then Matt inspects the foundation and notes the type, and whether it's poured, brick, fieldstone, or some other kind—there are many. He looks for cracks that could signal settling or crumbling, and also the condition of any areas that might need to be repainted. Foundation repairs can become expensive quickly, so he pays particular attention here.

Then Matt takes a step back and looks at the property itself. Is there fencing that needs repair? What is the overall condition of the front porch and driveway; are they well-kept and welcoming? Do the trees and landscaping need to be cut back or enhanced? At this point, we have to consider both what needs to be repaired and what needs to be updated in order to make the property suitable for our exit strategy, whether we plan to rent the property or flip it.

MAKE ASSUMPTIONS

Based on what Matt sees outside the house, he can make some assumptions about the inside. If the outside is very dated, the inside will most likely be dated too, especially kitchens and bathrooms. Since we can't get inside to confirm the condition, we generally make the assumption that we will have to reno these areas, and we use a standard estimate $8k for a bathroom and $15k for a kitchen. If there's carpet, we'll usually replace it. If there are wood floors, we'll often either refinish them or replace them with luxury vinyl flooring.

Finally, Matt considers the incidentals, so that he can prepare an estimate that includes the full scope of the work that needs to be done. Depending on the age of the house, are we dealing with sheetrock or horsehair plaster? Looking at the pipes coming out of the house can tell us a lot about the heating systems. Is there a high-efficiency heating system? Are there oil fill lines or a gas meter on the outside, which might suggest we're dealing with an original boiler or water heater? From experience we know that if we have to touch the electrical system, those updates can be expensive because we run into changes in building codes that require significant remediation. Then we must consider whether there's asbestos or lead paint, depending on the age of the property.

Matt will also call the local building department and health department to ask about what permits might have been pulled and closed out, which can give him an idea about issues like lead paint and septic systems.

CONSIDER THE COMPS

Especially if you plan to use the house for investment purposes, you'll want to assume that you'll make upgrades similar to your comps so that you can command the highest possible ARV. If the comps have granite countertops, then you're going to want to put in granite countertops. If they have vinyl siding, then you're getting vinyl siding. Do the comps have a slate roof or composite shingles? And so on. You add all those costs to make sure that the property meets the expectations for the area.

PREPARE THE ESTIMATE

Once you know what you need to do to the property, then do the research to find out what contractors typically charge in the area and estimate what the materials will cost. Call the GC that you found when you started building your network. Get a couple of expert opinions. Contact a building supply company or research materials and prices online.

Ideally you break down each element of the rehab based on your assessment of the property. Let's say you've gotten a quote to repair the roof for $300 a square—contractors generally quote roof repairs in 10x10 squares—and the property has a 20-square roof, so the rehab estimate is $6k. Then your quote for the kitchen is $12k, and the property has two bathrooms that will be $5k each. Paint, $6k. Redoing the floors, another $8k. Replacing the heating that's shot is another $7k. Then you just add it all up. The key is working with a contractor who can give you today's prices, unless you're a contractor yourself with the experience to know what things cost.

Another approach would be to consider whether the rehab will be light, medium, or heavy, and then come up with a rate per square foot for each of those categories. Maybe in your area, a light rehab runs $100 per square foot, while a heavy rehab runs $400. Multiply the square footage of the property by whatever category of rehab you plan, and then stick to that budget when the time comes to do the work. You can generally get a sense of the cost per square foot of an average rehab by talking to a general contractor. Every market will be different, obviously; rates in certain parts of California are a lot higher than in the Midwest where you can often get work done a lot cheaper. But a good contractor can tell you that the average cost for a heavy rehab—including plumbing and electrical—is $400 a square. If the house is 1,000, then you have a rough idea that that rehab will cost $40k.

COUNT ON CONTINGENCIES

Finally, we recommend you adjust your rehab budget for the additional risk of any missing due diligence or other unexpected issues that could come up.

For instance, you've done all your due diligence and you've come up with your rehab budget, but you couldn't get in touch with the city to confirm the last time the septic system was inspected or if it failed. Since you don't know for sure whether you'll have to replace the septic system, assume that you do. We recommend adding the cost of a new septic system to your budget. We know, it sucks, because that's maybe $20k you're adding to the rehab budget, which will lower your MAO substantially and means it's less likely that you'll win. If another bidder knows that the septic system is good, then you'll lose the auction. But we'd rather not buy a property with a hidden risk and lose the potential profit than buy it, find out we must replace the septic system, and be out $20k we didn't anticipate. All of a sudden, your margins get scary slim. When you're buying property for $150k to flip at $200k, an additional $20k can be the difference between a healthy win and a painful loss.

We will often round up our estimates to account for the unknown. If we think we can get the roof repaired for $12k, we may budget $15k just to be safe. But we also have a knowledge advantage since Matt is a general contractor. Assuming you're not a GC, another way to give yourself a little room for error would be to add a 20% contingency to your rehab estimate. If your rehab estimate comes in at $20k, add another $4k to it for good measure. If you ask any flipper, the average budget easily goes over by 20% to 30%.

Or maybe you decide to avoid this cost altogether by narrowing your search to a property that's turnkey. You won't have to worry about finding a contractor if you buy a property that's already fixed up and ready to rent or resell.

CHOOSE YOUR OWN ADVENTURE

*If you want to **understand other variables in the MAO calculation**, turn back to page 183.*

*If you're ready to **head to the auction**, turn to page 207.*

OTHER COSTS

Other costs include anything else that you might have to pay during the life of the transaction. The most common other costs in the world of foreclosure auctions include other liens, sales commissions for real estate agents if you plan to resell the property, and dealing with occupants.

Our advice for dealing with other liens is simple: due your due diligence before the auction to find out what all the liens are on the property! Being surprised by a lien due to incomplete due diligence can be a very expensive mistake. And when it comes to sales commissions, we typically don't try and negotiate too much. If we are getting our price for the property, we'd rather see everyone win on the deal, including the agent. For the most part, these costs are what they are.

Now if the house has people living in it, that's another story. You have to allow for costs associated with dealing with them, whether you offer cash for keys or pursue an eviction. If we see that a property is occupied, we always just tack on $5k to get the person out. That doesn't mean we always spend $5k, but we always include it in our cost estimates.

When coming up with the amount you should estimate, you'll want to take into account average rents in your local market along with typical moving costs. If the customary move-in fees in your market include first month's rent, last month's rent, and security deposit, estimate enough money to cover those costs for an average rental unit that's comparable to the property you're buying. You can assume the occupant will want to move into a home that's similar to the one they're leaving.

If the property has a bona fide tenant in it, which is a tenant with a valid lease, you'll probably be limited in terms of what you can do with the property until the lease ends. In that case, you have to figure in the impact of the lease on your holding costs. You may still be able to negotiate an early termination of the lease by offering the occupant cash for keys. Even if the occupant is a tenant with a lease, you could offer the tenant money—for instance, $5k—to break the lease. As long as both parties agree, almost anything is possible. If you think this option is likely, you'll want to include the $5k in your holding costs.

But since most foreclosures take longer than a year to come to fruition, there's a good chance the lease will be month-to-month by the time you close, or at least very close to the end. In that case, you may just ride out the lease. Let's say the tenant has three months left on their lease at the time of the auction. To be safe, maybe you assume it will take you only thirty days to close, so the tenant will have two months left when you become their landlord. Then assume the worst-case scenario: You give them a timely notice of nonrenewal, but they refuse to leave. You have to evict them. That process could add another three months or more. So now you're looking at five months before the property is vacant, so you'll want to include an additional five months of holding costs into your calculations, offset by the amount of rent you think you're likely to collect from this tenant.

CHOOSE YOUR OWN ADVENTURE

*If you want to **understand other variables in the MAO calculation**, turn back to page 183.*

*If you're ready to **head to the auction**, turn to page 207.*

PROFIT MARGIN

Unless you're buying the property as your primary residence, you need to figure a profit for you and your investors into the purchase price. We typically see investors command 20%-30% return on investment on deals where we're the wholesaler, because we also take a fee on the transaction. Between the investor's target ROI and our fee, the total profit margin is close to 40% or even 50%. When we're the investors, we target 40% to allow for the many unknowns that could erode our profit—but every investor is a little different. Do some research to figure out what ROI investors typically expect in your market, which is where networking with social media and other groups can be particularly helpful.

Obviously, the higher the margin you command, the fewer auctions you're going to win, so establishing your target return is both a personal preference related to your risk tolerance and a market consideration. On the flip side, if you're a homebuyer who doesn't need to make a profit at all because you're just looking for a home to live in, you'll be a very competitive bidder. Play with the MAO formula by reducing your target ROI to zero, and you'll see exactly what we mean.

CHOOSE YOUR OWN ADVENTURE

*If you want to **understand other variables in the MAO calculation**, turn back to page 183.*

*If you're ready to **head to the auction**, turn the page.*

CHAPTER 8

DON'T GET EMOTIONAL

We attend a lot of foreclosure auctions. A lot a lot. On average we've gone to dozens of auctions every week and hundreds of auctions every year. With thousands of foreclosure auctions under our belts, we've learned a few things about attending them that we'll share with you to increase your chances of success.

AUCTION DAY

Up until two years ago, 99% of the people at foreclosure auctions were professional buyers. We didn't see many buy-and-hold people, mostly flippers. But as affordable homes got harder and harder to find on the MLS and bidding wars drove up prices, we saw more and more prospective homebuyers.

Unfortunately, a lot of the homebuyers we talked to didn't know what they were getting into. For instance, most didn't know that there is a

120 calendar-day redemption period on federal tax liens, or that the redemption for tax liens is governed by state law. Few had done all their research or due diligence. Often they were getting in way over their heads—not all, but the majority. They couldn't find a house on the conventional market, so they were going to foreclosure auctions without really understanding how different this home-buying process is from the traditional route.

We've seen real estate agents bring their clients to foreclosures, give them advice, and then try to get a commission on the buyer's bid. Often the agents don't know what they're doing either. If you work with an agent, trust but verify their foreclosure credentials. Ask questions. Have they ever actually bought a foreclosure property at an auction? Can they explain the risks to you? Do they know how to research lien priority? Be skeptical of the answers, because people who really know about buying foreclosures can usually make more money doing it than they can advising other people on it.

That said, we do think it's a great idea to go to a foreclosure auction just to get an education on how they work. When Kev wanted to learn more about the eviction process, he sat in the housing court and watched a whole bunch of eviction cases. It was a great use of his time. We suggest doing the same thing to learn about foreclosure auctions. Go to an auction. See what happens. Ask questions. The hands-on experience of seeing the process first-hand is a great way to prepare for your first real auction.

Lienholders in judicial states must follow certain rules and get approved by the court to conduct a foreclosure auction. The process varies state by state, maybe even county by county. In some states, like Connecticut, the foreclosure auction happens at the property. Other judicial states will host it at the courthouse. You can drive by the property to check it out before the auction and then show up with the check in hand to bid on it at the courthouse steps.

Connecticut holds every single auction for all foreclosures across the state at noon on Saturdays at each property. Because all auctions happen at the same time across the state, it's really hard to attend multiple auctions. Interested bidders have to figure out in advance which one(s) they want to attend. Not every judicial state conducts their foreclosures this way, though. In other states, foreclosure auctions may take place at the property, at housing court, or even at the local town hall. You just need to know the process in your state.

In nonjudicial states, foreclosure auctions are generally held throughout the week. In Massachusetts, they're held Monday through Friday from 8 a.m. to 5 p.m. on the hour, every hour, sometimes even on the half-hour, at the property. If you're trying to get to a lot of auctions, you're running around the state.

The feeling at the actual auction can be different in different places. Where we live in Springfield, the environment is very casual. In Worcester and Boston, it's a little different. In general, though, nobody shows up in suits. Nobody is being overly formal. There's generally not a lot of interaction among the bidders because everyone's competing. Some people are chatty, but not talking about anything meaningful.

Besides the auctioneer and bidders, you may see a bank representative, although most of the time the bank doesn't show up. Matt has been to auctions where it was just the auctioneer and him. The auctioneer is usually approachable if you want to strike up a conversation or introduce yourself, although what they can tell you beforehand varies from state to state. In Connecticut, for instance, they can tell you the bank's minimum bid if the bank allows it; in Massachusetts they cannot.

But they're human, so if you build a rapport, they might give you hints and insights, especially if they like you.

And then there are times when the owner is at the auction too. Having an owner present at the auction can be disconcerting, to say the least. For some, it will likely be off-putting. But it might also give you an idea of who and what you'll be dealing with if you win, and it could even give you an advantage.

HELL HATH NO FURY

Matt was at a foreclosure auction, and there were a number of bidders. The bank was there as well as the bank's lawyer, all that stuff. Right before the auction was about to start, the owner came out of the house screaming, "Oh, this isn't going to happen. If you buy this house, I'm not leaving! I'm contesting everything!"

Matt wasn't fazed because we hear it all the time. And we get it. It sucks for the person losing their home. So the owner lashes out. It happens often.

The auction started anyway, and the bids went back and forth until another bidder won the auction. We came in second or third. But shortly afterward, the bank's lawyer reached out to Matt because the first buyer either couldn't or didn't want to perform. Maybe they got scared by the owner, which happens a lot when an owner comes out threatening like that. So, the bank then went to the next bidder in line, which was us. We bought it for our last bid price of $75k, which was only a thousand or so less than the original top bid.

Because Matt goes to hundreds of auctions every year, he's very friendly with the auctioneer. He's also very friendly with the banks. They know us. There are only so many auctioneers, and there are only so many banks. And Matt's generally a friendly guy—which is why we don't send Kev to the auctions because everybody knows he's not friendly.

Somehow the owner found out that we're all friendly and claimed collusion. She contested the foreclosure by saying that we were in on something shady with the bank. "Oh my God! They weren't the ones who won the auction." It was ridiculous. Who won the bidding was completely irrelevant. Most of the time it doesn't change anything from the standpoint of the owner, and especially if there's a deficiency between the winning bid and the lien amount. For instance, if the owner owes $100k to the bank, and there's only one mortgage, no municipal liens, no other liens against the property, and then it gets bid up to $120k—which sometimes happens—then the owner gets the $20k difference between the winning bid and the lien. But if there are other liens on the property, then the overage goes first to the other lienholders and then it goes to the owner. A lot of times, the owner gets nothing because there is a deficiency, which the foreclosure process wipes out. And in this particular case, there was a deficiency—so it shouldn't have mattered to the owner which bidder won the foreclosure auction because the homeowner wasn't getting anything from it.

When the owner legally contested the deal, the case went before a judge. We got named in the suit, the bank got named, the lawyer got named, the auctioneer got named. The owner basically hung us up for a whole year, even though we had already closed on the deal. We'd gotten a hard money loan so we could keep our own money moving, so our holding costs were mounting while we waited for the case to be resolved. And all that time, we couldn't risk putting additional money into the property in case we ended up losing, so any plans for rehab had to wait. In the meantime, the former owner was living in it without paying us anything for the privilege.

When we finally got in front of the judge, we were like, "We paid the money to close the deal. We paid back taxes, we paid everything. If she's going to contest the sale while she's living there, we should at least get a market-rate rent." It was a single-family home, three bedrooms, two baths, so we were asking $1,200.

But the judge basically said, "Nope. You can only recover your costs." Even though Kev argued that we had a hard money mortgage that we had to pay every month, the judge said no. He ordered her to pay only $250 a month for water, insurance, and property taxes—and only from that point forward. She didn't have to pay anything for the previous six months. She ended up paying about $1,500 to live in the property for a year, during which time we still had to service the house. Whenever she put in a maintenance call, we had to go out there to fix it.

Not every state is as friendly to occupants as Mass. But dealing with former owners and relatives of former owners is not for the faint of heart. If you live in a very tenant-friendly state and you're looking at a foreclosure with an occupant, our advice is don't take it on as your first property. Also, don't take it on if you don't have a lot of liquid cash because there's just so much risk involved. Most foreclosure buyers wouldn't take on the risk we do. The other two bidders in this deal dropped out.

If you have the fortitude and the financial flexibility, you can get a good deal, especially because occupied properties scare most folks. It took us a year to get the property free and clear, during which time we had to cover the holding costs. It did kind of suck, but we ultimately refi'd the property. Once it was vacant after that first year, we rehabbed it, rented it out, and then pulled out extra money, which we used for another deal. We still own it to this day. It's been cash flowing like a king. And that's all because we had the financial flexibility to make the deal work for us when everyone else walked away.

WEAR YOUR GAME FACE

A part of your bidding strategy might be walking around the property while you're evaluating it and talking loudly into a phone about all the issues you find. We do this when we're assessing properties before we bid. Matt will walk around with Kev on the phone and say things like, "Yeah, I definitely see asbestos through that window in the basement. Boy, that's going to be a big deal. We should adjust our bid based on that. And you know, we don't know yet if there's an IRS lien on this thing or not, so we gotta take that into consideration." We'll have our conversation about all the things we see—and maybe some of the things we don't—within listening range of other bidders.

Keep that in mind not only as part of your strategy, but also as part of what other bidders may use as their strategy. If they raise an issue you didn't research, you may want to pay attention. But if you've done your own due diligence and you're confident in your own research, maybe take what you hear with a grain of salt. It's all part of the game.

If you're a homebuyer looking to purchase a property to owner-occupy, remember that you likely have a pricing advantage over all the investors at the auction. If we were potential homeowners at a foreclosure auction, as part of our bidding strategy we would probably let other people there know that, especially if the other people are investors. Make it known that you're buying the property for yourself. Some investors—especially investors like us who attend dozens of auctions every week—won't waste their time hanging around to bid in an auction they're never going to win anyway. Maybe fewer people will end up bidding, and you'll save yourself some money.

On the flip side, be aware that other bidders might try to scare *you* away with that same strategy, only to turn around when they've won and say, "Ha! I think I'll keep this one as an investment after all!"

HOLD FIRM

If you've ever been to an auction, then you know it's easy to get caught up in the fervor of bidding: "Wow, this guy jumped up $10k! He must know something I don't know about this property. I'll bid just a little bit more. Okay, so I'll make a thinner margin. I'll still make money." That kind of thing happens all too often.

Our advice: Don't do it! Do not get emotional. Stick to your numbers. Don't go over your MAO. If you've been thorough in your due diligence and you've followed a disciplined process to develop your MAO, then trust your numbers. Otherwise, you can end up pulling the trigger on a bad deal. Remember that the whole point of buying property at a foreclosure auction is to get an undervalued property to increase your value and limit your risk. Don't blow it by overpaying now.

Sticking to your numbers can also help with game-day nerves. If you're hyped up on the day of the auction, remember that you've already decided what you're going to bid and what you're willing to pay. By the time you're at the actual auction, you've already decided to take the gamble of buying a home in foreclosure. The fact that you're now at the moment of truth shouldn't be more scary or more exciting or more stressful. You've trained for this moment.

The time to have been nervous was when you decided with your business partner or your life partner to put your hat in the ring. That was a couple weeks before the auction, when you were looking at houses. Being stressed on auction day is like being stressed on the day of your wedding. You've been engaged for months, you set a date, you made plans. It's not like "Surprise!" you've got a priest in front of you. Unless you eloped to Vegas.

THE TWO GUYS TAKE ON FORECLOSURE AUCTION STRATEGY

- Buyer Beware
- Stick to Your Numbers
- Don't Get Emotional

HOW TO LOSE MONEY FAST

One of the best ways to lose money fast is to approach the foreclosure auction with a gambler mentality, dollar cost averaging properties based on faulty information. We once had a partner who bought properties with that faulty mindset. He just kept dollar cost averaging our purchases based on bad information. He would look at Zillow and see a property's estimated worth was $300k. Then he'd say, "Listen, we bought it for $100k. According to Matt," (who only saw it from the outside for five minutes) "it needs $50K worth of work, so we made $150k today. Woohoo!"

And then he would buy the next property and he would say, "We could bid this much. Let's keep bidding higher!" He'd go to an auction, and we'd be on the phone with him. The bidding would hit our max bid number. And he'd get all excited, "You know what, let's just bid $10k more. We made $150k this morning so we can afford to bid a little higher on this one." We thought that was the dumbest way in the world to look at our max bids, but we bought into it. We got sucked into this faulty line of logic.

We can imagine somebody at a casino thinking the same thing. "Listen, I won a pretty good hit on a slot machine earlier today. I can afford to lose a few grand on blackjack. You know what, I got some overtime at work. I can cover my mortgage. No problem. I can spend a little bit more today in the poker room." It's such a dangerous path. You really need to be set on your MAO before you go to the auction, as if you were going to a casino. Put whatever you're willing to lose in your pocket and don't spend any more. Prepare yourself beforehand to stick to your numbers.

You've got to be firm in your thinking, "My maximum bid is $50k. I'm not going to bid $75k. I'm not going to end up getting excited in the moment and bid up to $80k. My maximum bid is $50k."

Then when the bidding goes over $50k and you don't win the auction, you just watch the rest of the auction play out. Or maybe you turn and get into your car and drive away. Go to the next one.

Real estate is a very inefficient market. Making a profit takes a long time. It's not like stocks where you can buy them and turn right around and sell them and—boom, boom, boom, boom, boom—make a quick profit. You buy a property and have to digest it. It can take a while to see a profit from it. So, treat each deal as if it's in its own bubble. Don't start co-mingling and dollar cost averaging because you never know what's going to happen. You need to wait for the closing. Once you get into it, you find out it's going to need a new stack and there's $2k you didn't count on spending. And then, oh, the contractor doesn't show up for a month. So now you've got an additional $5k in holding costs that you weren't expecting. So many things can go sideways. It's just better to treat each deal as its own individual bubble.

The whole process is usually over in less than an hour. In Massachusetts, they have up to an hour after the time the auction is supposed to start to complete the bidding. So, if it's supposed to start at 1:00, they have until 1:59 to finish the auction. Typically, as long as the auctioneer gets to the property ahead of time, the auction is done in five to ten minutes.

CHOOSE YOUR OWN ADVENTURE

*If you **lost the auction**, turn to page 305.*

*If you **won the auction**, turn the page.*

WINNING!

Well, you did it! Congrats on the W. Now, don't take your eyes off the ball.

On the day that you win the auction, you'll hand over your deposit, sign a memorandum of sale or a purchase and sale agreement, and give the auction company your attorney's information so their attorney can contact yours later. If the auction is in a judicial state, that document will go back to the court for the judge's review and (you hope) approval. If it's a nonjudicial state, the auction company will bring the document to their closing attorney.

You do not have right of access to the property until your deed is recorded when the sale closes, generally thirty to ninety days later. You don't walk up to the door and start securing it. You don't start boarding up windows. Most sale agreements specifically say you don't have the right to the property until the sale closes, and you can lose your deposit if you step on the premises or if you try to go into the premises before you own it.

That said, once you've won the foreclosure, you're legally liable to close the deal when the bank is ready to close with the property "as is." Let's say that in the time it takes for you to close on the property, there's a flood, or a natural disaster, or a fire, or somehow the condition of the property substantially changes. It's still in "as is condition" when the time comes to close the deal, even though it's not in the same condition it was in when you won the auction. You are still "required to perform," which means you as the buyer are required to take ownership of the property.

One way to limit your losses would be to just walk away from the deposit. Most of the time, the deposit is at least $5k, which is a lot of money for a lot of people. Maybe that's all the money you have in the world to buy a property, and you may not want to walk away.

The other way to limit your losses would be to insure the property as soon as you have a contract to buy it. Once you've won the auction and before the deal has officially closed, you have what's called an "insurable interest." You put a deposit down and you have a contract to purchase, and therefore you have an interest in the property that is insurable. A lot of people don't know they can talk to their insurance broker as soon as they win the auction and get insurance on the property that will protect them from loss.

If you've bought a home before, you may remember that you were required to show proof of insurance before you closed. If you're borrowing money to finance your purchase from a foreclosure auction, your lender will most likely require proof of homeowner's insurance at the time of closing here as well. Insuring the property right after you've won the auction just moves the timeline up several months.

We recommend that you get insurance for the full value of the property, at least what you actually bid if not the full ARV. Your insurance broker can tell you what's available based on the specifics of the property. Here's why: Let's say you won the property, you got insurance on it as soon as you won the auction, and then there was a fire. You could make a claim to recover your loss even before the deal formally closes.

ALWAYS USE PROTECTION

We've seen all sorts of strange and crazy things when we've bought homes through foreclosure. This case here of a guy with a porn studio was kind of a classic example of a house-hack. He owned a three-family house. He lived on the first floor, since many people invest in a multifamily to live in one unit and rent out the rest. He rented the second and third floors out to two different tenants. From what we understand, one of them made home porn in the basement in lieu of rent. It was a makeshift "studio," and not a properly finished basement. It was not a nice property. It was just a little area of the basement with a mattress and some lighting and a curtain.

Then, of course, there was a falling out between the landlord and one of his tenants. She said either "I can't pay rent" or "I won't pay rent," and he said, "Then I'm gonna kick you out." To which she said, "Well, then I'm going to complain to the city about the conditions here! Oh my gosh, I've got kids!" So, the city came in and said, "Why, look at all these citations for code violations we've got against you!"

Because of all the code violations, the owner stopped getting any rent. Fast forward: He lost the property, and we won it through a foreclosure auction. We remediated all the code violations and brought it back into compliance, including issues in his own apartment. Then he refused to leave, so we had to pursue an eviction. We finally got him evicted just like everybody else who refuses to leave.

But before he left, he stripped everything from the property. You've heard people say, "They took everything but the kitchen sink"? Well, he took the kitchen sink. He took the walls; he literally took out the drywall we'd just installed. He unscrewed it and took it down. He took up flooring. Every single light fixture was gone. The toilet was gone. He stripped the apartment, just gutted it. He took everything. Everything. We're talking about a property with a market value of $700k, and he did at least a couple hundred thousand dollars in damage.

Luckily, after we won the auction and while the deal was still pending, we'd gotten the property properly insured. When we tried to work with the owners shortly after we won the auction, we were able to get inside the house and take full photos. So when we found the damage after the deal closed, we were able to make a claim and show our pictures to the insurance adjuster. The insurance company paid our claim, which protected us from the loss. We were still able to fix it (again) and sell it for a profit.

The takeaway is that as soon as you have a contract, you have an insurable interest that you need to protect. Talk to your broker the day you win the foreclosure to secure your coverage, and then send the insurance policy to your attorney. Don't wait a week. Something could easily happen that day or maybe a day or two after the auction—which is why we also take photos the day of the auction. If you can't get inside, take photos of the outside and through the windows to document the condition as of the time of the auction. We recommend insuring your interest as soon as you win the auction.

What happens next depends on where you live.

CHOOSE YOUR OWN ADVENTURE

*If the property is located in a **nonjudicial state**, turn the page.*

*If the property is located in a **judicial state**, turn to page 225.*

AFTER THE AUCTION IN A NONJUDICIAL STATE

Often when we buy foreclosures, the lienholder says they plan to take thirty days to close. More often than not, they run into title issues or other complications. While many deals do close in thirty days, some end up being six months before they close.

The most common reason for delay is title issues, which the lienholder must cure before they can sell the property. More and more frequently, another cause of delay for us in Massachusetts is due to a former homeowner contesting the foreclosure. When this happens, the lienholder, the auction house, and even the winning bidder can end up in the middle of a lawsuit for months or even years.

When the lienholder is finally able to close, the winning bidder must fund the remaining purchase price over and above the deposit or else risk losing their deposit. When the deal closes, the winning bidder receives the deed and, at long last, can now access their property.

CHOOSE YOUR OWN ADVENTURE

*Now that **you're a homeowner**, turn to page 229.*

AFTER THE AUCTION IN A JUDICIAL STATE

The closing process in judicial states is administered by the court, and the court has to approve the winning bid. Compared with nonjudicial states, the process is actually a lot cleaner as a result. There is less reason or opportunity for anyone—particularly the former homeowner—to contest the foreclosure.

First, disclosure: We have a lawyer who handles the judicial review process for our purchases in Connecticut, so we don't claim to be experts in all the possible inner workings of the process. But we do know that after the foreclosure, a committee of lawyers representing the state administers it. After the auction, the committee goes back to the judge and requests a hearing to review the validity of the foreclosure process and the winning bid. They typically notice your lawyer as well.

At the hearing, they'll review the winning bid. Let's just say the winning bid was only $40k on a house worth $1M. The judge can deny the sale, saying that basically it wasn't a proper or fair foreclosure. Maybe there was a huge hailstorm the day of the auction, and you were the only one who showed up. As a result the property sold so cheaply that the sale is not fair to the homeowner. The judge could order a redo. This happened to us when we bought The Fortress in Wilton, Connecticut (see chapter 1 for the whole incredible story). There was only one other bidder besides Matt. After we won the auction for a small fraction of the appraisal, the judge deemed it questionable and ordered a new auction—where we won it again.

Hindsight being 20/20, we should have let that one go.

Essentially, the judge determines whether the foreclosure auction produced a reasonable sale. They're looking out for all parties involved. The lienholder has rights. The owner has rights. So, all their interests must be protected and considered. The judge is making sure nothing drastic is outstanding, and no one is making an aggressive case saying, "I was cheated here by the way this foreclosure process went down." The judge wants to make sure everyone got properly noticed, and everyone received the relevant documentation. They want to exhaust every possibility that the foreclosure was somehow unfair, inappropriate, or invalid to ensure that the process is clean so it properly wiped the slate with regard to this property. All interested parties had an opportunity to speak and to get notice. If the judge is inclined to deny the winning bid and order a new auction, there's another process.

In the case of Wilton, as an example, first there was a hearing to review the auction and the winning bid. At that point the judge was like, "I'm looking at this. It seems like it went for far less than the appraised value. How can you justify that? We need a new hearing so you can make your case as to why I should let this transaction go through or deny it." Then he scheduled another hearing for several weeks later. In the meantime, Matt went to the property and took pictures to document the rough condition it was in. He worked with our attorney to write up a whole justification of the price we offered. We submitted that to the court before the second hearing, where our attorney argued our case—to no avail. The judge denied our bid and ordered a new auction. At that point, we got our deposit back, but we were out all the lawyer fees.

It usually takes another sixty days for the new auction to take place, and then the whole process starts over.

Eventually, though, the judge will approve the foreclosure process and the outcome of the auction, even if it takes several tries.* Once the court approves the deal, the lienholder sets a closing date. On the closing date, the winning bidder must fund the remaining purchase price over and above the deposit or else risk losing their deposit. When the deal closes, the winning bidder receives the deed and, at long last, can now access their property.

CHOOSE YOUR OWN ADVENTURE

*Now that **you're a homeowner**, turn the page.*

*We've never seen a homeowner successfully sue to take back possession of their property during this process, but hypothetically we guess it's possible. Stranger things have happened.

CHAPTER 9

LOOK FOR THE WIN-WIN

Congratulations! You closed the deal. You're the proud new owner of a foreclosed property. You did as much due diligence as you could. You're confident it's the ideal property to fit your game plan. Now the *real* work begins.

Most of what you'll do next depends on whether the property is already vacant or currently occupied, except for one thing that we highly recommend you do at this point: get title insurance. Title insurance protects your ownership of the property from defects in the title. Remember all that title research? If something was missed, title insurance will protect you as the owner from a resulting financial loss. It's in your best interest to get title insurance as early as you can, because it's a lot of risk not having it, especially with foreclosed properties. You might not be able to get a policy on an occupied property, but then again you might.

GENIUS STUPID

In 2016 and 2017, we ran into an issue getting title insurance on several occupied foreclosure properties. The workaround our attorney came up with when the first one happened was to ask the occupants to sign off on a document saying they would never raise any claim that we didn't own the property. It seemed really stupid. We thought it was a fool's errand when we got what the attorney wrote up for us.

"Get these people to sign this document," he said, "And then you guys are in good shape."

That was all we needed to know. Kev went over to the property and had a conversation with the occupants, since it would solve the title insurance problem if he could get the occupant to sign. And he did, which was bananas.

Some ideas are stupid, and some ideas are genius stupid. Don't be afraid to consider genius stupid ideas when you run into roadblocks, even if you need to pull in someone smarter than you to do it.

Now you're at a crossroads, so proceed with caution.

CHOOSE YOUR OWN ADVENTURE

*If you now own a **vacant property** (you think), turn the page.*

*If you now own an **occupied property**, turn to page 237.*

VACANT PROPERTY

First, you want to take special care to confirm that the property you own is really vacant. We've been fooled before—several times. At least a few of those times didn't end so well for us.

If the property is vacant, we immediately go over to secure it. We change all the locks in the doors immediately, just in case the former owner still has keys. We lock all the windows that can be locked. We take tons of photos and videos to document the condition of the house. We get as much documentation as possible so that if the condition changes, say the occupants vandalize it or a fire starts, we have proof of the condition for an insurance claim. This precaution has saved us quite a few times.

You might be tempted to immediately change all the utilities into your own name as soon as the deal closes. After all, that's what you do when you buy property the more common way, right? But we've learned the hard way that before you do that, you must be *absolutely certain* that the property is indeed vacant. Sometimes it can be hard to tell, especially if you haven't been able to get access inside the property before the auction or even before the deal closed—which happens 99% of the time.

If the house is actually occupied and you move the utilities into your own name, you are now likely to be on the hook for paying them without compensation from the occupants. Remember, the occupants didn't pay their mortgage. They're not likely to pay you for the utilities. If you subsequently try to force the issue by turning off the utilities, you could be accused of what's called "constructive eviction." It happened to us.

UNCONSTRUCTIVE EVICTION

This mistake we made became a disaster. We bought a property at a foreclosure auction. The yard was a shambles. The house was distressed. We believed it was vacant when we bought it. We noted it down on our records as vacant. We bought it; we closed on it.

When we close on a property, we go through some basic procedures. Somebody in our office creates a report that says we own 123 Fake Street, vacant, utilities are on or off, the heat is oil or gas or whatever, that kind of stuff.

So we went through our process, and we shifted the utilities into our name. It was wintertime, so of course we wanted to make sure the pipes weren't going to freeze. Our receptionist called up the electric company to start the process, "Hey, we gotta get our heat on at this property. We've gotta make sure the pipes aren't going to freeze."

She went down the list and changed all the utilities over into our name. And then we discovered, oh no, the property was occupied. The people were just living in a dump. Kev tried to reach out several times to connect with them, to no avail. Then we're like, "Well, crap, we're paying for electricity for these people who won't answer the door, won't talk, and won't leave. So darn it. We're shutting it off." We figured they'd put the utilities back in their own names.

So, we shut off the power. But legally, that looked like a constructive eviction, like we were trying to freeze people out of a property in the middle of wintertime. Then their lawyers were like, "What the hell are you doing? Oh my gosh!"

We were like, "Okay, sorry. You gotta put the utilities back in your name then."

And they were like, "Based on what? Why should we have to put it in our name? Look at the sanitary code."

Turns out the sanitary code basically says that all utilities are included at a property unless there's a lease agreement stating otherwise. And, of course, we didn't have a lease agreement with the former owner of the property; they're not our tenant. But they demanded: "You must have known the code, and you did the right thing originally by putting the utilities in your name. Then the second they give you an answer you don't like, you punish them by trying to shut off the power."

We were like, "No, we thought the place was vacant!"

They were like, "That's not how it seems to us. It seems like you knew the law was to have utilities in your name. Then she wouldn't move out. You didn't like that. She was going to exercise her rights and go to court as she's fully entitled to do, this disabled single mother. You didn't like that. So you shut her power off in the middle of January, you heartless SOB."

And we were like, "No, no, no! That's not how it happened! We'll turn the utilities back on in our name as a show of good faith. We will show up at court. In the meantime we'll put them all back on in our name today. But we'll show up at court, and we'll have our eviction hearing. We'll go through the process, and the occupants can exercise their rights and we'll have it heard by a judge."

And of course, then that got dragged out. Meanwhile, we were paying to heat the place. Of course, the tenants then ran space heaters for all their heat because the power was free. So they heated the place on our dime for hundreds of dollars a month while the eviction process dragged out and out and out.

So, lesson learned: Do not change the utilities for your new property into your name until you are absolutely certain that it's vacant.

Matt has a checklist we go through once we've acquired a truly vacant property—which is usually the ultimate goal before we kick off the next strategy. At this point, our investments have followed every strategy in this book and then some.

TWO GUYS TAKE ON A POST-CLOSING CHECKLIST FOR A VACANT PROPERTY

- Make certain the house is truly vacant!

- Change the locks on all exterior doors.

- Take pictures of the property inside and out, and store the photos in a safe place. We like to use Google Albums for free picture and video storage.

- Perform a health and safety inspection and plan to repair any issues ASAP—you're now responsible if someone gets hurt!

  - Check that smoke detectors are present and functional.

  - Check that all doors are secure.

  - Check that all windows are locked.

- Confirm heating fuel type and amount.

- Take pictures of all utility meters, including meter numbers.

- In winter months, confirm that property is winterized to prevent pipes from freezing.

- Check for any animal entry points (you don't want to have to evict a family of raccoons).

- Change all the utilities into your name.

- Draw up the complete scope of work for the rehab, if one is planned.

- After the rehab work is done, execute the exit strategy (occupy, rent, flip, etc.).

CHOOSE YOUR OWN ADVENTURE

*If your new property is truly **vacant and ready for the next step** in your game plan, turn to page 301.*

*If you've discovered that **your property isn't vacant** after all, keep reading.*

OCCUPIED PROPERTY

Apparently you are not faint of heart. Or maybe you're just really surprised. Either way, you now own an occupied property, which means your first order of business will be dealing with the occupant.

Whatever else you do, you have to go into this stage of the process expecting that it's going to take a little time—or maybe a lot of time. When you're dealing with a person, you have no idea what will happen. Even when you think you know what will happen, you don't. You can't even take them at their word. Don't say, "Oh yeah, the situation is all taken care of" until you have the keys and a signed release of claims in your hand. Trust us.

You're now headed into Bizarro World. The occupant will look you in the eye and say, "Yeah, I'm moving out next week. I'm almost packed." They're going to say…whatever, and then the second something doesn't work for them, you'll be the first person to suffer. If somebody in the situation is going to suffer, they're not going to lean on their family. They're going to lean on *you*, so all bets can be off at any point.

Negotiating with the occupant may not always be a gauntlet, but it's almost never a walk in the park either.

SECURE THE PROPERTY

In Massachusetts, once we own a property, we're responsible for everything that happens on and in it. That means if the residence is occupied, we have to make sure there is running water. We need to make sure the smoke detectors are installed and working. If not, it's our responsibility to fix those problems. It's all state law stuff. You have to have a "habitable property" if somebody's inhabiting it. And if there's no running water, we gotta fix it. And if there are no smoke detectors, they need to be installed. If the property's vacant, it needs to be secured. So we have responsibilities to secure the property the moment it's legally ours.

If the property is occupied, securing it can be harder than you'd think. We've had to get temporary restraining orders against occupants who refused us entry to the property to conduct an inspection. Another tenant denied us entry claiming she was disabled with anxiety, so we had to take her to court to negotiate entry.

TWO GUYS TAKE ON A POST-CLOSING CHECKLIST

- Knock on the door to make contact with the occupant and complete the safety inspection.

- If you can't do an inspection that day, set up a time soon to return and conduct it.

- If no one is home, post a notice that you will return the next day to introduce yourself, change the locks, and inspect the property.

- Perform the health and safety inspection and plan to repair any issues ASAP—you're now responsible if someone gets hurt!

  - Check that smoke and carbon monoxide detectors are present and functional.

  - Check the heating fuel type and amount.

  - Check for electrical hazards.

  - Check for hoarding issues.

  - Take full property photos inside and out, including utility meters.

- Get names and contact info of all occupants.

- Discuss with the occupant their plan to vacate, and negotiate your next steps.

- Draw up the complete scope of work for the rehab, if one is planned.

- After the rehab work is done, execute the exit strategy (occupy, rent, flip, etc.)

A LIEN IN WINTER

It was a foreclosure in a very remote town. It had been a bed and breakfast, and it had a barn and a decent amount of acreage.

Often in smaller towns in Massachusetts, very few bidders show up to foreclosure auctions, and that's always a good thing. Less competition. So one day in July, Matt showed up at the auction to find no other bidders. Just the auctioneer. Matt walked around the property and came across a note on the barn indicating that it was occupied. He thought, "That's weird." Looking through the windows of the main house, he could see it was vacant. He didn't think much more about the note. After looking around the property and checking out what he could see of the house from the outside, Matt ran the numbers. He figured the ARV to be $420k and the rehab budget to be $35k.

The auctioneer opened the bidding. Since Matt was the only bidder, we quickly won it for much less than what we'd been willing to bid, $193k. We were all excited.

Right after the auction ended, we didn't technically own it yet, but we did have an insurable interest. So, Matt wanted to get a little bit better look at the house since it was obviously vacant and in the middle of nowhere. Technically we're not supposed to go into the property until after the closing, but he went inside and found mostly abandoned stuff. Then he heard a noise coming from the kitchen.

He walked over to check it out: The kitchen was flooded under six inches of water. Mold had grown everywhere. The pipe to the washing machine had split. Because the house was on a well and the valve to the well was open, the water was pouring in. The leak had obviously been going on for a while. Matt went down into the basement and closed the water valve to stop the problem from getting worse. Then he shut off the breaker. He didn't think it would be a big deal to shut everything down. Mostly he just wanted to make sure that the water wouldn't get turned back on by a trespasser wandering through the vacant house.

He started thinking about the repairs as he headed home, still excited about the win. "We need to rip out the floor. We have to remediate the mold issue." And so on.

A day or so later, we got a call from our lawyer.

"What is going on?" our lawyer was asking us. "Did you guys go into the property??"

Our lawyer had gotten a call from the bank's lawyer, who'd gotten a call from a lawyer representing a dude who, as it turned out, had been living in the barn with his girlfriend. Typically with foreclosure auctions, the winning bidder is not supposed to make contact with the owner or any of the occupants until the bidder legally owns the property. They're not supposed to go on the property. And we know that. But we figured there was no harm in turning off the water since the property was vacant. Or so we thought.

The dude living in the barn thought differently. He was flipping out. So, Kev went out to the property to introduce himself and try to smooth things over. He didn't find the dude, but he turned on the well again. He also found a garden hose supplying the barn with water—never permitted, all done illegally. We knew we'd be in for a treat when the deal finally closed, since it appeared we had a squatter.

Then it became fall, and it was getting cold in Massachusetts. We started worrying. How the heck was the dude still living in the barn? It wasn't a habitable place! How was he heating it? He could use a space heater and cause a fire, and we'd be responsible. He could light a fire that could get out of control, and we'd be responsible. We had to do something. We had to talk to the dude.

The house wasn't exactly along our normal daily route, so it was a pain in the butt to drop in regularly. Kev had to go to the barn several times before making contact, but eventually succeeded. Kev was prepared to start the conversation much like he does in these scenarios, but perhaps slightly more aggressive. After all, the dude was not the former owner. He was not even living in the house. And he'd been pretty evasive so far. This time when Kev knocked on the barn door and stepped back, the dude came to the door.

"Hi. My name's Kevin. I heard that somebody is living in my barn, so I'm trying to find out what's going on."

The dude acted like he had a hard time hearing.

So, Kev said, "Come outside and have a conversation with me."

"Oh, okay," the dude said, and kind of teetered outside.

Kev suddenly realized "the dude" was just a doddering old man. He was polite. He was even kind of charming. Kev went from being like, "I got to go over there and lay down the law" to "Wow, this is just an old timer."

Kev learned that the old man's sister was the former owner of the house. At some point, she had converted the barn into a three-season guest quarters that she listed on Airbnb before she let the old man live in it with his longtime girlfriend. Kev didn't go inside, but he found out they had a couple of baseboard heaters and a little electric fireplace. They had jury-rigged a bathroom shower that wasn't insulated. The place wasn't meant to be used in the winter, but the electric heaters were enough to keep the chill off. It was clear that the arrangement hadn't happened just recently. According to the old man, he and his girlfriend had lived there for maybe seven years. And he was a veteran.

Finally, Kev told him, "We can't let this situation continue. We can't have you living and sleeping in a place that's not technically habitable. It's not safe. How the heck did you live here during the winters? How have you been living here for so many years?"

And he was like, "Well, it gets really cold."

He said they compartmentalized the barn down to a small space by hanging up blankets and then cranked the heat up. But the heat would escape right out of the uninsulated walls. Obviously, it was a sad situation.

Even though he really empathized with the old man, Kev told him that the arrangement couldn't continue. The barn was not meant to be lived in year-round. His sister had owned the house, but she had passed away. That's how the house went into foreclosure. But Kev could only push so hard. The old man was an elderly veteran. Kev wasn't going to call the cops and say, "Hey, this guy's living in our barn. He's going to burn the place down, get him out right now."

Instead, we decided to do what we could to connect both him and his girlfriend to services. We now have a lot of experience working with the elderly and with veterans, and so we could work with an elderly veteran. Kev started calling all the agencies he could think of to coordinate services for the old man. He arranged for the directors of several different government agencies to call each other and figure out a plan for the old man. Within a couple days, state officials promised Kev they would get personally involved if local services didn't make a plan for permanent housing.

A representative from the U.S. Department of Veterans Affairs met Kev at the property, in the hopes of aiding the old man. But the old man didn't want to engage with any of the community services agencies. He was very nice and good natured, but also disabled and really scared.

"I don't want to go," he told Kev. "I don't know where I would go. I've been here so long, and this is my sister's place, and...."

It was so difficult and sad. He just didn't want to take the VA's help. And he absolutely refused our help. Kev even tried to put him up in a hotel that we paid for. Once his girlfriend learned that Kev's name was on the credit card guaranteeing the room, they walked out of the hotel and would not stay there.

If he had worked with the VA program, the old man would have been immediately eligible for an emergency housing placement in a hotel and then permanent housing assistance in a unit with heat, water, and a kitchen. But Kev could not convince him to accept the assistance. The old man was polite, but refused. He went back to putting his head in the sand. It was incredibly frustrating and heartbreaking.

By January, we had to move ahead with the eviction. It was winter, and the barn was no longer remotely habitable. The garden hose providing water to it was bound to freeze, and then the old man and his girlfriend would have no water and almost no heat. So, we went to court.

When we went before the judge, a representative of the VA appeared as a witness. Kev testified about the services he had worked to coordinate for the old man and his girlfriend. He described the assistance that had been arranged with the VA and other local agencies. Kev also explained that the old man's living situation was not safe. It was not a home. But the old man had hired a legal aid attorney to represent him, who argued that the barn was habitable. The judge ordered the city to inspect the property, since the two sides disagreed about the conditions.

It took weeks, but the city completed its inspection and reported back that there were no dwelling permits for the barn. There was no kitchen. According to the city, the barn was not a dwelling. The legal aid attorney argued that the old man previously had access to the kitchen in the main house, and that his rights to use the main house should be restored. We argued that the main house was condemnable, especially after the weeks if not months of flooding in the kitchen. We also argued that the old man, as polite and kind as he was, was not a tenant. There was no record that he had ever rightfully been a tenant on the property. He had no lease. There was no record of any payment by him or his girlfriend. He had no legal right to use the barn, let alone the main house, as a dwelling.

The judge ultimately agreed with us. He urged the old man to take advantage of the services available to him. Then the judge ordered him to leave the property. At that point, we were able to get the old man to agree to accept the VA's assistance. It was the dead of winter by then.

We agreed to store his belongings at the property as long as he didn't live there. As long as he stayed off-site, we would hold onto his stuff, and he could have access to it as he needed. He took his personal belongings, and we held onto his longer-term storage items. But then we could stabilize the property, shut water off, and winterize the main house so that the pipes wouldn't freeze.

Several weeks later, the court contacted us again. The old man had showed up there complaining we had locked him out of the property, and he couldn't get his belongings. He should have contacted us for access. But since he didn't know how to communicate electronically, he went to court instead. When we went before the judge—again—Kev explained that the old man just needed to contact us. Kev gave him the lockbox combination.

The judge issued an order that we were to store the old man's belongings until the end of March and could throw away anything he left behind after that. So that's how he ended up wrapping it all up: He came, got most of his stuff out, and left a bunch of junk behind. We threw away a thirty-yard dumpster's worth of trash.

It took about $20k and hours and hours of time for nearly six months, trying to negotiate with the old man, before we were able to resolve the situation and acquire the whole property vacant. We could probably have done it faster the hard-charging way. But none of us wanted to do that. Had we tried, a judge might have come to the old man's defense and leaned on us to do even more at a higher cost.

It did cost us, though. Our plan for the property had been to wholesale it immediately after we closed on the purchase. We had to hold off, and our partner in the wholesale business was like, "Come on! We gotta get this guy out right away! We gotta sell it!" Fortunately, we had the financial capacity to take the approach we did, but if we had just started out with real estate investing and this had been our first property, it could have killed us financially. It could have cost us everything.

If this foreclosure auction had been our first, we probably would have called the cops. We probably wouldn't have had the financial wherewithal to negotiate for nearly six months or offer the old man a hotel. If we were not real estate investors but instead homebuyers, a judge might have admonished him that we were not a resource for him. We were regular people that bought a house to paint and fix up and move into. Maybe his attorney would have argued for him differently. Maybe his attorney would have urged him to work with VA earlier on.

Or maybe not.

LEARN THE RULES

When it comes to dealing with occupants, it is absolutely critical to either know—or, if you don't happen to be a lawyer, then hire a lawyer who knows—the housing laws and specifically the landlord-tenant laws in your state. We've become very familiar with the laws in the two states where we operate, and in the meantime we've made some very expensive mistakes. Our best advice is: Hire an expert in your state before you make the mistakes that will cost you time and money.

One reason is that the laws governing former owner-occupied properties may be different from the laws governing tenant-occupied properties. Different states handle possession, tenancy, and housing laws very differently, so talk to a local lawyer who specializes in landlord-tenant law for advice about dealing with the occupants of a foreclosed property.

Then, go to court. Watch the process. In Massachusetts we have actual housing courts, that is, courts that are literally just for housing matters. There are juvenile courts, family courts, regular district courts, and then there are housing courts. You can go and watch these cases be heard. And we gotta tell you, at least where we live, when you go watch these cases, it's like having seats at the *Jerry Springer* show. It's insane. It is straight-up entertainment. People walk in wearing Cookie Monster pajamas. It's the craziest stuff.

Wherever housing cases get heard in your state, it's public. You can go attend court. When we first started out, Kev literally hung out at housing court for days and just watched cases. It was a great way to get a feel for what the judges expect, what satisfies judges when they have questions. We've seen bad landlords—and there are plenty. It's good to see what a judge thinks a good landlord's responsibilities are; whether or not we think it's fair doesn't matter. Whatever the judge thinks, those are the rules you're playing by. It doesn't matter what's written in the code book. If the judge wants it a certain way, then, darn it, that's the way it's going to be.

And different judges handle things differently. So that's the other thing: If the judge changes in your case, you need to adapt your strategy. Yes, the law is the law. But at least where we live, judges use their powers of discretion very often. Judges are human. They are not all alike, by any means. So you want to know how the particular judge in your case leans on the issues they're deciding.

You have to know how to play the game. The best way we've found to learn the rules, other than hiring a lawyer to handle everything for you, is to watch from the sidelines. So go to court. Take popcorn.

KNOW THE PLAYERS

In most states, having a former owner living in your property is different from having what's called a "bona fide tenant" living there from a legal standpoint. A bona fide tenant is one with whom there is an arm's length agreement for reasonable consideration; in other words, payment of rent close to market rate. The agreement doesn't have to be written; lots of bona fide tenants have verbal agreements with reasonable consideration that are perfectly valid. Your relationship with a bona fide tenant will be landlord-tenant, and it will be governed by your state and local landlord-tenant laws.

A tenant who's not bona fide does not have an arm's length agreement with reasonable consideration. Often these folks will be the uncle, sister, cousin, or son of the homeowner who pays $300 a month for rent in a home that should rent for $1,100 a month. Maybe the owner wrote a lease two days before auction for $5 a month for twenty years because he knew he was losing the house. No unbiased, unrelated person will look at that situation and consider it reasonable. That's not a real lease, because the owner signed it only to screw the new owner and help out a relative at the same time. A judge would likely not uphold that lease if you had to sue for eviction. Your relationship with a non-bona fide tenant is more like business-customer, and it will often be governed by different laws than the state and local landlord-tenant laws that govern bona fide tenants.

START TALKING

Whatever path you take to resolve the situation with the occupant, the first step is having a conversation with them so that together you can make a plan. For some foreclosure buyers, that's going to be pretty awkward. When that time comes, you'll want to have your proof of ownership in hand so you can show the occupant that you have the deed to the property and you are now the rightful owner. You'll want to be able to explain what has happened to the property from a legal standpoint and show them proof.

One of the main goals of this first conversation is to figure out who you're dealing with. Are they the former homeowner? Are they a bona fide tenant with a valid lease? Are they just a squatter in a property they thought was abandoned? Once you know whether you have an actual landlord-tenant relationship with the occupant or not, there are actually quite a few ways to negotiate a solution.

CHOOSE YOUR OWN ADVENTURE

*If the occupant is a **squatter**, keep reading.*

*If the occupant is a **bona fide tenant**, turn to page 258.*

*If the occupant is **the former homeowner or other non-bona fide tenant**, turn to page 260.*

SQUATTER

You just closed on the property you won at a foreclosure auction. The first thing you do is drop by your new property only to find it's now inhabited by squatters. And by this we mean people with absolutely no legal right to be in the property. They're not even pretending they have a lease. They're just breaking and entering, and then setting up camp. People don't like the word, but we would call anyone who's in your property without your consent, without any kind of consideration—money or work or something being exchanged—a squatter.

WHAT DO YOU DO?

Treat them like you would if you came home from the grocery store and found a rat in your house. You own the property, and somebody who clearly doesn't belong there showed up and took up residence. Whether it's a rental property you've owned for ten years or a foreclosure property you've owned for one week, you go to your property, walk across your front lawn, march up your front steps, put your key in your front door, and you open it. Maybe you hear a noise inside. You're going to be, well, you'll probably feel a lot of different things. Everybody reacts differently. But if you're not scared of them hurting you, then they should be scared of you hurting them. Because what are they doing in your house? You never said it was okay.

There are parallels between squatters in a foreclosure property and squatters in a rental property. You treat them the same. You talk to them, you call them out, you encourage them to leave. Usually they do.

"GET OUT"

Kev was at one of our rental properties once looking for a deadbeat tenant named William who was several months behind on rent. He lived in an apartment on the first floor by himself. We hadn't seen him for a while. He wasn't returning calls. Kev had been forced to chase him down for rent before. But now, whenever Kev went to the apartment, either no one would answer or only other people would answer, like a girlfriend or random friend. Which was fricking weird.

As Kev was walking down the street toward the building, a person he didn't recognize walked past him into the common area entrance of this eight-unit building. The guy was pretty rough around the edges. He didn't look like somebody you'd want walking into your place. So Kev slowed up and observed him for a few moments. The guy walked into the common area and toward the locked door going into the main part of the building where there's a buzzer. Tenants can open that door with a key, or guests can push a buzzer for a tenant to let them in.

Kev approached him as if he was just being helpful. He opened the door with his key and asked, "Are you trying to get in?"

And the guy was like, "Oh, uh, yeah."

Kev said, "Do you have a key? I've got a key."

"Oh, no," the guy said. "I just, you know, I'm just here, you know, for my friend."

So, then the guy took a prescription bottle out of his knapsack. He had only been in the hallway for fifteen seconds. It's not like he had been there, buzzed, waited, and then gave up on his friend. He was all too willing to just leave the second Kev said hello to him, which doesn't track as normal, right? Immediately, that was a red flag for Kevin. So, he pushed the issue. He was live-streaming and posting the video on social media as it happened.

Kev asked innocent-sounding questions but got more aggressive as the red flags kept popping up.

Then the guy was like, "I'm here to see, you know, a friend."

Kev said, "I can let you in if you wanna just go knock on their door."

"No, that's fine. It's fine," the guy said. "He's not there."

The guy started to make his way out of the building.

Kev asked, "You weren't here long. What friend was it? Who are you looking for? Because I'm looking for someone who owes me rent. So if this guy's your friend, you know, I also wanna talk to him."

And he's like, "Oh, no, you know, no, it's okay."

Kev pushed the issue. "Well, what apartment were you buzzing?"

And the guy answered, "I don't know. I just know which button to push on the buzzer panel."

"You don't know what apartment you were here to visit? Well, what is your friend's name?" Kev asked.

"You know, uh, you know, his name is, um, I think it is William," the guy stuttered.

"You think your friend's name is William?" Kev asked. "Okay, well I'm looking for William too. I was actually just knocking on his door. When was the last time you've seen William? What's going on with him? Tell William to call me because I'm looking for him too."

And he's like, "Okay, I'll tell him as soon as I see him."

Kev said, "Yeah, please do. He owes me a lot of money, so I really wanna talk to him right away, as you can imagine."

"No, I got you, boss," the guy said. "I haven't seen him for a while."

"Okay, well hopefully you see him before I do," Kev said, "because he owes me a lot of money. You understand what I'm saying?"

The guy shuffled on back down to the end of the street where he came from and where there's usually a lot of panhandlers.

The next day, Kev was back out at the property looking for William. Since the property was empty again, he went inside the apartment and saw that the power was out. The fridge was disgusting. Clearly nobody had been living there for quite some time. Kev posted a notice of abandonment on the door that said we were going to change the locks in seventy-two hours and the tenant should reach out to us if this was an error. We will work it out.

Kev went back again the next day to check on it. He turned on his video. Then he knocked. Nobody answered. Pound,

pound, pound. No answer. He used his key to go in, looked around the corner, and this time a few people were lying on the bed in the bedroom. A guy was sitting in a chair. Another guy was spread out on a couch.

Kev said loud enough for everyone in the apartment to hear, "Who the hell are you? What is going on here?" Since he was obviously recording, he started livestreaming it as well.

They tried to give Kev some BS story. "Oh, we're friends with William. We didn't know he didn't pay his rent. We didn't know."

Kev was like, "I got strangers here. My tenant's gone. You guys are here, nobody's paying. There's only partial electric. This place is filthy. I don't like this at all. Get out."

"Yeah, we'll leave. We're not looking for a problem, you know?"

"Okay," Kev said. "I'll come back at the end of the day around dark; make sure you gather up whatever you're taking with you. Once you're gone, I'm changing the locks. Please don't be here when I get back. I don't want to have to handle this differently, you know what I mean? Please, let's just have you be gone when I come back. Do I need to call the cops?"

"No, no, no, no, no!" they said. "We'll be gone."

"Great," Kev said. "Now get out."

And that was that.

Usually when challenged, people will roll over. A challenge can be as simple as talking to someone. The difference between someone shoplifting at a retail store and not shoplifting could be as simple as an employee saying, "Hey, how are you? What can I help you with today? I'll be right over here if you need me. I'm only a step or two away." The effectiveness of that simple little interaction is partly why Walmart has greeters, to help shoplifters understand that somebody is paying attention. Somebody's there, somebody's present, somebody's always around. As soon as they realize that's happening, a lot of times squatters will do the best they can to remove themselves so they don't have to deal with a bigger problem.

If you need to call the police for assistance, we recommend that you call them in advance and prep them on the situation. Let them know that your situation involves criminal trespass and not a landlord-tenant issue. If you make an emergency call for help, they'll probably be reluctant to intervene when they show up. It's a roll of the dice. Sometimes the police aren't very well versed about who's in the right and who's in the wrong in these situations, so they'll quickly say, "Listen, this is a civil matter. This is not a criminal issue. They're living in your house. If you believe they should be evicted, then you have to go through court. We don't handle evictions."

CHOOSE YOUR OWN ADVENTURE

*If you were **able to get the squatter out** and the property is now vacant, turn to page 301.*

*If you have to **pursue an eviction**, turn to page 288.*

BONA FIDE TENANT

Generally speaking, foreclosures do not wipe out bona fide leases. If a tenant signed a bona fide lease with the former owner, they are legitimately a tenant with a right to stay in the property until the lease ends. If the tenant has paid consideration and the agreement is arm's length from the owner, then their lease is still valid after the sale closes. That means that if your intention is to get a vacant property, you as the new owner of the property must either honor the lease or try to buy the bona fide tenant out.

The first step is to knock on the door and have a conversation. Typically the conversations go something like this.

Kev will knock on the door. When the tenant answers, he introduces himself and lets the tenant know he's the new owner. He asks the tenant what their plan is. Often the tenant is surprised that the property has been foreclosed on, and that Kev is the new owner.

Then Kev will say, "I know this is weird. I'm sorry that you've been renting a place that got foreclosed. But I bought it with the intention of fixing it up and selling it. I know you have a lease. What's your plan after that? Were you planning on moving somewhere else? Is there a chance we could talk about ending your lease early? What could I do for you to make that happen? Could I buy out the rest of your lease to make it worth your while?"

At that point, you hope the tenant says something like, "Give me $10k and I'll move next week! Yeah, that's cool with me. I was going to move in six months anyway. I'm a single person. I'll move next week. No problem." If they do, then you can negotiate the termination of the lease in exchange for cash.

But it doesn't always go like that. So, that's when you can offer money to help with the inconvenience of the transition: "I'd be happy to give you $5k." Maybe you'll end up paying $10k, but the point is that you can almost always negotiate anything at any time as long as it's mutually agreeable. More often than not, you can negotiate with a bona fide tenant to end a lease early in exchange for cold, hard cash.

Before you hand over the cash, have the tenant sign a release of claims. Work with an attorney to get a release of claims that will protect you *before* you offer cash so that you're going into the conversation with the release of claims and the cash. Then give them the cash only after they sign the release and give you the keys as they're ready to vacate.

Now, if the tenant refuses and continues to honor the lease by paying you rent, you're riding out the lease. But after either a little more time or a little more money, you've got yourself a vacant property.

CHOOSE YOUR OWN ADVENTURE

*Now that **you've got yourself a vacant property**, turn to page 301.*

FORMER HOMEOWNER OR OTHER NON-BONA FIDE TENANT

By the time a foreclosure auction has happened, most owners have a pretty good idea of the situation with the property, but often one of the first things an owner asks for is proof. So again, make sure you go to the property with the deed in hand so that you can go through the process of explaining what has happened and how you became the new owner.

Most of the time when you talk to the former owner, they will deny any knowledge of the situation. They will stonewall. They'll say something like, "I don't know anything about anything about anything." Once the occupant declines to engage, there isn't much to be done in that moment.

The goal of a lot of our encounters with occupants is to help them realize: "It's real. You lost the house. It's mine, not yours." You have to push the boundaries a little bit more each time. Each time Kev interacts with the occupant, he's a little more aggressive, a little pushier. On the first visit, he might respond to the owner's denial by saying something like, "Okay, well, while I'm here, I'm going to walk around the property. I'm going to take pictures of the back of the house and the yard and the condition of everything."

The occupant may respond, "I don't want you on my property."

Kev's response might be, "Well, I don't really want *you* on *my* property. So you understand where I'm coming from: We have the same problem here. But I'm going to do it anyway."

Then Kevin will finish the walk-around over the occupant's protests. Periodically he'll stop by again. He'll pull right into the driveway like he owns the place (because he does). He'll take more pictures of the outside, maybe make a phone call loudly in the yard. He just keeps driving home the point that *it's real*. The foreclosure happened, and they're going to have to confront the situation at some point. They have to stop stonewalling.

We deal with occupants of all the foreclosure auctions we buy the same way. When we take over a property after a foreclosure auction, the second Kev sets foot on the grass or the walkway up to that house, he feels like he's home. This is our house. He doesn't necessarily start off super aggressive, but he starts off with that mindset. He won't be an absolute jerk or be very aggressive about it. But he will use the mindset of The Rightful Owner when he approaches the occupant.

If he walks up to the house and somebody is in it, his first question is, "Who are you? What are you doing in my house? I didn't know anybody was living here. I just bought this place in a foreclosure auction. Obviously, you've known for a while that this day was coming. You're not even packed? Why are you still here? What's your plan? Because I've got contractors ready to come in and start work renovating the place. I was here today just to change the locks, make sure the smoke detectors are installed, and confirm everything's ready for my guys to start working."

Even if the person has lived there with their family for twenty years, Kev still adopts that mentality because it drives home exactly what the scenario is for the people still living there. Kev "assumes" that they just need a couple more days to pack up and leave. He assumes they will say, "Oh, you know what? Sorry about that. We were moving out last week and then something came up, but we'll be out by this weekend." That's what Kev is looking to hear, and he makes it understood by the questions he asks and the tone of voice he uses. Why would somebody still be in our house?

People usually react one of two different ways: 1) deer in headlights, or 2) grizzly bear. The deer in headlights types will say something like,

"What do you mean? I didn't know there was any foreclosure. My wife was the one who paid the mortgage. I don't understand any of this." For that reason, Kev brings a copy of the deed with him when he visits the property the first time, knowing full well that the cops might get involved. When the cops get involved, the first thing they will want to know is, who owns this place? The deed is critical because Kev doesn't necessarily have a key to the door. He doesn't have mail delivered to the property or any of his stuff inside the house. He could be a drifter showing up, knocking on the door and being like, "Hi, I own this house." So he's the one with the burden of proof. He anticipates that.

He also must nullify what the occupant usually says, which is, "I didn't know anything about this. I have to see proof. Nobody told me anything." With the deed in hand, Kev can say, "No problem. I don't know how you didn't know about the foreclosure auction that took place months ago. It's very public. There's even a notice in the newspaper. But here's the proof right here that I own the property, if that helps. It's kinda weird that you need it. You can verify this online; you don't need to take my word for it. But here's a copy of the deed, which you can go online and look up." That tends to take the wind out of their sails.

Sometimes the occupant will say something like, "You'll have to come back next week after I talk to my attorney and when I can talk to someone official who can show me proof that you own this place, because I don't believe it."

Kev will push at that point to overcome any objections they raise and fast-track their departure from our property. "No," he'll say. "Here is the proof right in front of you. You don't need to go anywhere to confirm it. It takes five seconds to review the document in my hand. You can verify it right now while I'm talking to you."

The occupant could be the owner, or it could be a sister or son who never moved out, even though the owner died five years ago. They just never left and never paid the mortgage. Kev has had people tell him, "I rent this from my uncle" or "I rent this from my sister" or "I just keep the place up and they let me live here for free," even though the place is obviously a dump. When that happens, Kev will reiterate, "I'm not doing that anymore. We bought the property to [flip/rehab/rent/whatever]. You knew this must be coming. What is your plan now?"

Kev keeps trying to get the conversation back around to "what are you going to do now"?

Kev will often hear "I was just going to stay here because nobody's come here and said anything to me yet. I haven't gotten any paperwork showing that the ownership changed, and nobody's talked to me about this. So until that happens, I'm just not going to do anything because I don't know anything."

In that case, Kev will respond, "Well, I'm here to tell you this is happening. I own this house. It's happening. Now, what is your plan? Where are you going? How long is it going to take?" And then he'll start talking about getting access to the property.

It starts becoming real for people when you show up at the door and have that conversation. But it really starts becoming realer when you walk through every room of your own house—every bedroom, every bathroom, the attic, the basement—opening closet doors and walking around like you own the place. Because you do. Nothing hits home more than that. So to make that happen, Kev will say, "I need to come in now. I want to take a look at what I bought here."

The occupant might say, "Come back next week when I've had a chance to talk to some people about this."

Kevin doesn't cave. "I don't know what that means. You've had years to 'talk to some people.' I'm not putting this off another week. What if the house catches fire this week? What if it explodes this week? What if somebody dies because of something wrong in the property this week?"

"Nothing's going to happen," they'll say. "I've lived here twenty years. Everything's fine."

"That's great, but I have strict liability here, and I want to make sure whoever's here is safe. I need to make sure nothing bad happens because if a first responder has to come out, they're going to look to me because I own the house. They're going to hold me accountable for it, not you. You know? So, I need to come in and do a safety inspection and walk through and see what I've got. And if you don't let me do this, here's what I'll have to do. I don't wanna do this, but I'm going to have to go to court and file a temporary restraining order against you for access into my own house. I will do that. I've done it before. This isn't my first time doing this. I don't wanna do this. You're gonna end up paying the expenses. So what is the harm in me coming through and making sure that your family has smoke detectors working and no gas leaks? What's the harm in that?"

The idea is for Kev to get into the property. It is important to make sure it's safe. But really the main objective is to walk through your property, helping them understand that it has happened. It's real. And here we are. Those are the deer in headlights people.

The other people are the grizzly bears. The ones who try to dominate the conversation, the ones who are belligerent and slam doors on you. The ones who threaten, "I'll burn this place to the ground! You're not coming in here. You wanna come in here? You're going to have to go to court. I'm the boss!"

As with a deer in headlights, you have a conversation with the grizzly. You explain exactly what the bottom line is. You try to be as matter-of-fact as possible. Keep in mind that when you're in court or in the newspapers, they're going to say that *you* threatened *them*. So you are not threatening. You are simply stating, "If you don't do this, here's my only recourse. I don't want to, but I will take you to court. A judge will order you to let me come in and perform a full inspection of this place. I don't want to do that, but you're not leaving me any options. I own this place."

Occasionally the former owner will pack up and peacefully leave. It happens sometimes.

LIKE A GOOD NEIGHBOR

Once when we won a foreclosure auction, we were prepared for a legal fight after Kev went and talked to the former owners. They were denying, denying, denying that the auction happened. "I don't know anything about this. I don't know what you're talking about," yada, yada. They were like, "Well, nobody said anything to us about this place being foreclosed."

And Kev was like, "Well, this is me saying that we now own it."

Then when he installed our company sign with our company contact info on the front porch, which is something we do on all the properties we take over, a neighbor across the street flagged him down. Kev chatted with her for a while and was able to get inside information about the property. She'd been dealing with issues with the previous owners for some time, including an unresolved drainage problem on her property which Kev promised to resolve.

A few days later, the neighbor called us up and said, "Looks like those people who were living in that house are packing and moving out right now." So we went over and, sure enough, they had moved out without a word to us. We didn't have to go to court. They literally did the right thing, which almost never happens. They just decided to leave after Kev told them we'd bought the house. A week later they were gone, and we found out because Kev made nice with the neighbor who then called us with the news.

If we hadn't made that connection, there's a good chance it would have been a week or more before we'd known the house was vacant. The backyard was really well secured. The shades were all pulled. So, it really comes in handy having good relationships with neighbors and making sure that your info is posted once you win an auction.

Unfortunately, if you have a former owner-occupant living in your property and you don't want them to stay but they're not willing to leave, the only way to remove them is to go through an eviction process. An eviction process is the legal way to get an enforceable order for them to leave.

We don't like to pursue evictions for a variety of business reasons—never mind that we're decent human beings. But business-wise, it takes time. Time is money. It takes money and lawyers and legal fees. We don't want to do things that cost our business money. No business does. We're also nice guys, and we don't want to drag families with kids into the court where they'll get thrown out of the house they've lived in for the last twenty years. We'd rather reach a mutual understanding and a mutually agreeable solution instead of throwing it in front of a judge who says, "Hey, listen, everybody out of the pool."

Before you go down the legal route, you may be able to negotiate a less adversarial solution. We make every possible effort to avoid it ourselves by working with former owners as much as we can. A less adversarial solution doesn't always start out that way. We've had people insist that they need six months before they can move out. Or they'll insist that, "you can't kick me out. I'm in a protected class! I'm disabled. I talked to a lawyer about this."

In that case, Kev's response is "Listen, I'm not sure what you told them about this situation, but you're confusing what a *landlord* would have to do. I'm not your landlord. You're not my tenant. You're…"—and maybe Kev uses the word squatter, but squatter escalates it. Kev doesn't like escalating unless he's in a situation that calls for it. But if the former owner is yelling, then he's like, "Listen, you're a squatter. You're talking about a landlord-tenant relationship. That's not you and me. You are living in *my* property. You are the *former owner*. You don't have tenant's rights. This is what I can legally do, and I don't want to have to do it. But if you don't do the right thing by leaving when you don't own the place anymore, then you are forcing me to go through the eviction process. I don't want to do that. That's why I'm having a conversation with you. If I didn't want to have a conversation with you, I would've just sent you the paperwork yesterday when we closed on the house. But here I am, trying to give you the shot to do the right thing by leaving the house you no longer have a legal right to occupy. If you don't want to negotiate with me, then I'll freaking leave. You'll get the paperwork, and then you're going to be tossed out faster than you can imagine."

And it's not fast, but it *is* faster than they might imagine. Kev doesn't exaggerate the length when he's talking to them either.

He tells them, "Listen. It's a three-day notice to vacate. After that, we send you a summons to court. You have a right to be summoned. You're going to have a court date scheduled. It's usually about a month or so after our first notice. So I'll start working on that notice tomorrow. You'll get it in a few days. Then we'll have court in about a month to a month and a half. And at that point, you're going to be standing in front of a judge. I'm not sure what you're planning on telling him. You don't pay rent. You're not my tenant. You're not protected by tenant laws. You don't own the house. I have the deed. I don't know how you think you're going to win that case, so you're going to be asked to leave. And once that happens, that eviction goes on your record for an incredible amount of time. I rent apartments to people for a living. I look at their records. And if I have ten other people applying that don't have an eviction on their record, guess what? I'm not taking the person with an eviction."

If they haven't shut you down and they let you keep going, that's the kind of stuff you can say to help them understand the situation. You have to be very clear in what you say and very careful about how you word it, though, because later in court they'll recount your conversation to the judge by saying, "He said I'll never be able to rent a house again. He threatened me." Kev is careful not to use words like "you'll never." He'll phrase it like, "If I'm a landlord and I see an eviction on a person's record, I won't rent to them." That doesn't mean "you'll definitely never find a house." But that's often how they will represent it.

So now it's time to get creative. Almost no idea is too crazy to try. Over fifteen years, we've come up with some pretty crazy ideas ourselves. Maybe one of them will work for you.

CHOOSE YOUR OWN ADVENTURE

If you're **willing to consider a crazy idea**, turn the page.

If you're **not a fan of crazy ideas** and want to take your chance in court, turn to page 307.

A CRAZY IDEA

In our experience, this crazy idea works. Why? Because money talks.

One way to change the dynamic when you're dealing with a reluctant occupant is by offering what's called "cash for keys." How do you get somebody to be willing to do something they otherwise won't do? Pay them cold, hard cash.

We don't personally like this practice much because it essentially rewards people for doing the wrong thing: They're living in a property that they don't own without paying for it and refusing to do the right thing, which is *leave*. But we also have to look at it from a business standpoint. Once again, don't get emotional!

You may be able to get the former owner out of your house and save yourself so much time and money versus going through an eviction process, which usually takes months. Some people will leverage this dynamic and use it against you, but it's important to understand the tradeoffs in terms of your time (which is equal to money) and hard dollars in terms of lawyer fees and court costs, not to mention the risk of being countersued by the former owner. By paying cash for keys, you're fast-forwarding the process of taking possession. If pursuing the legal remedy of an eviction will cost six months and $5k, maybe you can offer less than that and resolve the situation in a couple days or weeks.

We don't like it, but we do it.

NICE TRY

Be prepared for the people who pretend they've lived in the property for months or even years because they think cash for keys is a legal requirement when there's been a foreclosure. They think it's a Real Thing. We've had people demand, "Just gimme your information about the cash for keys program."

"What information?" Kev will say. "I'm just some dude who bought a house. Do you think I have, like a pamphlet? I don't have a pamphlet. I have a business card. I bought a house. I'm a guy with the money to buy this place. All of a sudden, you're saying you live here. Nobody lives here. There's been no water or electricity for six months. You don't live here."

"Yeah, I do. That's my stuff."

"You moved out six months ago. You heard somebody bought it. You walked down the street with your old key that still worked and now you're like, 'Tada! I live here. Give me money.'"

And that's what people will do. They'll absolutely do that. There's a vacant property, a 100% vacant property, and they'll come out of the woodwork saying, "What are you talking about? I've been living here forever!"

When this happens to Kev, he takes the person at their word— and then asks for some proof so he can write them a check. Can they produce a copy of their lease? No? How about a piece of mail with the property address on it? No? Or a driver's license or ID with the property address on it? No? How about a neighbor who has one of those things who's willing to vouch for them?

No? Golly. Kev would sure like to help, if the person could help Kev out with something to show that the person lived where they say they lived. Usually fakers will scurry away by this point. But if they don't, sometimes Kev will still offer a small sum to make the person go away—$100 and the offer, "Let me give $100 for your trouble. Having to move must be really difficult. If you sign this release, I can give you $100." It may not be the $10k jackpot they were hoping for, but it might put the conversation to an expedient end.

Just remember: If you're giving money to anyone, always have them sign a release of claims first.

Every market is a little different, but you're probably looking at $5k or $10k to get the occupant to release their claims rather than dig in and basically squat for two years. Banks usually pay about that much when they offer cash for keys, and it's become so commonplace that people now think it's a legal requirement. When we've had that first conversation with a former owner about their plans to leave the property, we've had people say, "Okay, so where's my cash for keys? You've got to give me money if you want me to leave."

"Dude, you're now living in *my* house," Kev will say. "The right thing would've been to leave already. What's your plan now? I can give you a couple weeks."

"That's ridiculous!" they often respond. "We need to find a place to go! We don't have any money."

"You've lived here for ten years without paying anybody," Kev will answer. "You knew the place was auctioned three months ago. You knew this day was coming. These things don't happen overnight. You must have thought about your next steps. You must have money saved."

You'd be amazed at how many people have done nothing when we have this conversation. Our goal is to move them from nothing to something. And soon.

When it comes down to getting occupants out of your house, people need two things: They need a place to go, and they need a way to get there. Help them find an apartment. If you own other properties like we do, maybe you have another apartment for them. If you don't, you can still help them find another property they can move into. If you can't do that, you can give them some time, and you give them the money for the first month's rent, last month's rent, and security deposit—whatever is typical in your area—along with the actual moving costs.

When you're negotiating their exit, you're essentially coming up with the money to overcome their barriers. In exchange for that help, they agree to leave without countersuing you for anything that they can make up. And that's cash for keys.

AS GOOD AS IT GETS

Kev just wrapped up one where it went swimmingly. The occupant was open to talking from their first conversation. The whole way the deal went down was very unusual because it all worked out, and she was honest. That almost never happens in our experience.

Kev went to the property and knocked on the door. When the occupant opened it, Kev started his usual spiel: "Hi, there. I know this might be kind of awkward. You don't know me. My name's Kevin. And, well, basically I'm the new owner of the house. And as you probably know, it was foreclosed on, and there was an auction a few months back."

"Oh yeah, no. We know," she said. "We were just waiting for somebody to come."

"Okay," Kev said. "Since you knew this day was coming, and it didn't happen quickly, you must have a plan?"

"Honestly, we were just trying to ride it out for as long as we could and get through the holidays here, before somebody came by and told us we had to leave," she said.

"Okay, well, yeah, I'm that guy," Kev said. "So now, like, what's your plan?"

She was polite about it, so Kev danced around the word "eviction." He didn't want to set her off to the point where she wouldn't negotiate.

"Okay, well listen," he finally said. "I can definitely work with you. It sounds like you were kind of planning for this. So how much time do you think you need?"

She wanted a couple of months.

Kev declined. "Well, no, I don't think that's fair or reasonable, but I can maybe talk about a couple of weeks, you know?"

So, what he worked out with her was that we would provide boxes and tape, and then reimburse her for the cost of a U-Haul. He also agreed to cut her a check for $750 once she left. We even put a dumpster out there.

> They put all their junk into the dumpster. And whatever stuff they wanted, they took with them. Then they broom-cleaned the property. So, we didn't really have to pay a contractor much at all to do the clean-out afterwards. We saved a good chunk of money.

When you offer cash for keys, have the occupant sign a release of claims first. They're agreeing to drop their guns, and you're agreeing not to put them through an eviction process. Again, we'll stress that you should work with an attorney to get a release of claims that will protect you *before* you offer cash so that you're going into the conversation with the release of claims and the cash. You're settling a legal dispute with each other. Then give them the cash only after they sign the release and give you the keys as they're ready to vacate.

The release protects you from future disputes over the occupant's belongings. By signing it, they agree not to come back and claim, "Where are all my Picasso paintings? Or, I told you I was coming back for three laptop computers I left behind. You stole them." The release is an acknowledgment by both parties that you're waiving all claims with the understanding, "We're done here."

You might feel like the victim in this situation. You might be thinking, "*I'm* being taken advantage of by somebody who's squatting in *my* property. What do you mean settling claims? *I'm the one* with a claim! I should be over there taking care of business!" We get it. But you have to realize that, fair or not, many of these folks are going to have legal options that will cost you a lot of time and money.

So, think of it this way: It could cost you $20k in holding costs and legal fees plus a year and a half of time and frustration to win an eviction case. Why not just give them $5k to resolve the issue in a month? It's just giving your lunch money to the bully. At least you don't get a black eye. It's crazy, but it's usually much cheaper and more efficient.

CHOOSE YOUR OWN ADVENTURE

If **cash for keys worked**, congratulations! Turn to page 301.

If **cash for keys won't work** and you want to try an even crazier idea, keep reading.

If you're done with crazy ideas and want to **take your chance in housing court**, turn to page 307.

AN EVEN CRAZIER IDEA

So, the occupant is digging in. Maybe you don't have enough liquid bank to buy them off, or maybe they just can't be moved. Don't give up yet!

If you're buying the property as an investment anyway, then one of your moves could be simply to rent the property back to them. Believe it or not, we've done this a number of times: We've taken over an owner-occupied, foreclosed home and rented it right back to the former owners. In most cases, they continued to live in their homes as tenants for years and were very happy with the arrangement. Several owner-turned-tenants rebuilt their credit as our renters and went on to buy houses again.

You might be asking, "Well, they didn't pay their mortgage and now you think they're going to pay the rent? Why would you trust that?" But everyone's situation is different. Sometimes life throws you a curveball. Maybe the person lost a job short-term, which meant they couldn't afford the mortgage. And then the bank fees on top of the past-due mortgage payments were too much to overcome. Now that they have reliable income coming back in again, they can come up with a security deposit and the first month's rent. Sure, they lost the house to foreclosure, but renting it is appealing because they no longer have to worry about the ongoing maintenance—the roof repairs, the heating system, the property taxes, the insurance, maybe even some of the utilities. They can just focus on paying one bill, which is the rent they pay to you, and being a great tenant in the house they've lived in for years.

You'll still want to screen them like any other tenant. If they have the financial wherewithal, keeping them in the house as tenants could be a solution made in foreclosure heaven because you're both getting what you want: You're getting an investment property with good tenants and they're getting to stay in their home. We know it sounds crazy, but it works!

If one of you is not up for a long-term rental arrangement, another work-around is to sign a short-term lease with the very clear understanding that the intention of the agreement is simply to give the occupant a little more time to make a plan to move out. Kev's had so many of these conversations with occupants now that it's second nature.

"I can give you some time to move. Usually when we buy properties this way, people have already moved out. I don't know what your plan is, but I can give you a few weeks. I can work with you. I can help you relocate, give you cash for keys. In the meantime, I need you to sign a lease saying that we took over the place. We're obviously the owners now. So here. Sign this document saying that you're aware, and I'll work with you as best I can. I don't want to have to go through an eviction process with you, and because you just lost your house to foreclosure, you're not going to be able to go buy another house right away. If I must go forward and do an eviction—which I unfortunately have a lot of experience with—you're probably going to have a hard time renting with an eviction on your record. So, sign this document saying that I clearly own the place. If you don't give me a hard time, I'll be able to give you some leeway."

Sometimes Kev has been able to do that without offering any money, just giving the people a week or two because they were already moving. Some people then just did the right thing and moved out. Other people didn't have a place to move to and didn't have a solution at all. When that happened, Kev sometimes offered to rent the house back to them long-term.

"Maybe we could work it out where you just rent it from us and we could let you continue staying in this home," he'd say. "You've been in it for ten years raising your family."

Surprisingly, it has actually worked for us several times—although it didn't always end the way we expected.

ALWAYS A ROLLERCOASTER

We have long-term rented back to the owner a property we just won at auction more times than you would think. In one case, the former owner's kids never knew that a foreclosure happened while they continued to live in the house for years. We did a very good job of letting everybody believe it was still their house. When we first made the agreement, the guy asked us not to say anything to his kids. What did we care? We didn't have to be part of their daily lives, so we didn't post our company sign on the house. If we did any work on it, we acted like he was hiring us as contractors.

The situation wasn't without its challenges, though. The guy had a pool that the neighbors kept complaining about. At one point, code enforcement was calling us, because neighbors reported him to the city for not keeping the property up. So, we cleaned up the pool and did some landscaping around it. Then he was so mad that we cut down a tree. It wasn't "his" tree anymore. But he was like, "That was an expensive tree!"

Kev told him, "I'm sorry, but the tree went with the sale of the house. We did everything to avoid this."

Still, he rented from us for a few years and was generally a good tenant. Until he burned the place down. Then we leveraged the insurance payout to buy a two-family house, which we renovated and sold for a master profit.

Be aware that if you go this route, you are changing the nature of your legal relationship with the occupant from business-customer to landlord-tenant. Even if you don't sign a lease, even if you agree only that the occupant will pay you $1k each month for three months so that they have time to make other housing arrangements, you have agreed to rent them a residence. You are now a landlord, subject to all the landlord-tenant laws where the property is located. If you end up having to pursue an eviction at the end of whatever lease term you've agreed on, the tenant has different rights than they would have as a squatter. They now have the right to bring a counterclaim against you.

You may get tired of us saying it. We get tired of saying it: Hire a good housing attorney with expertise in landlord-tenant law to advise you before taking this step. If you're going to take money, it has to be understood that the exchange of consideration does not create a tenancy. In Massachusetts, it's for what's called "use and occupancy" only, not rent. We make it clear that the occupant is not paying us a thousand bucks in rent. They're paying a thousand bucks for "use and occupancy" for the next sixty days, or whatever term we agree to, so that when the inevitable happens and both sides go running to the judge, you have documentation: "Judge, what do you mean she thought she was renting the place? It says right here in bold print: '**This does not create a tenancy.**' We were not renting it to her. How is there any misunderstanding about that? This is not a case of 'he said, she said.' We put it in writing, and we both signed it."

This option works really well if you do it right and use an attorney, but it can be fraught with peril if you don't. You must get a good housing attorney to advise you, or you risk expensive mistakes.

CHOOSE YOUR OWN ADVENTURE

*If this **crazy solution worked** for you, congratulations! Turn to page 301.*

*If becoming the former homeowner's landlord was a bust but you're game to try **a stupid-crazy idea**, turn the page.*

*If you're done with these crazy ideas and want to **take your chance in housing court**, turn to page 307.*

A STUPID-CRAZY IDEA

First, well done for having the intestinal fortitude to try yet another crazy idea. Clearly, you're in it to win it, and we think that commitment will serve you well. We told you this game is not for the faint of heart, but it *is* for the bold of spirit. You're here because cash for keys didn't work, or becoming a landlord to the former homeowner didn't work, or you're an overachiever who's reading every page of this book if it kills you. We don't care why. We're just glad you're here.

So, the craziest idea of all is so crazy, it's stupid-crazy: Sell the house back to the occupants.

"Sell it back to them? Are you nuts?" you might ask. "Can you really sell the house to the person who just lost it in a foreclosure?"

Well, yes. And yes. And we appreciate your skepticism. Even former owners are surprised when we suggest it. Sometimes they tell us we're laughing-crazy and insist they won't pay us a dime more than we paid at the auction. Then when we walk them through the offer, they very quickly realize that they could land a huge windfall, too. And we usually offer this option as just one of the four we're sharing with you.

This is how it works: Not everybody living in the house was necessarily on the mortgage. Maybe the mortgage was only in the husband's name and the wife has a good income, or vice versa. Maybe another family member is living with the person who held the mortgage. So while the person who held the mortgage was foreclosed, the other occupant wasn't. It's one of the most obvious answers. It's right there in front of your face, but most people never think of it. Check the deed. Then check the foreclosure documents. Compare to see whether everyone on the deed is listed on the foreclosure documents. If not, this solution might just work.

We've done this multiple times, where the husband's name was on the mortgage and he got foreclosed on. The wife also had a good income, though, and she was working. Sometimes the couple actually saved a bunch of money while they weren't paying the mortgage once the property was headed to foreclosure, so they had a down payment for the purchase. And the wife didn't have a foreclosure on her record, so she was able to buy the house.

Here's how everybody wins: Let's say the mortgage note behind the foreclosure was $200k. You won the foreclosure auction for $100k. You sell the home back to a relative of the former owner for $150k, assuming the house appraises for that amount—which is likely if it appraised for at least the amount of the previous mortgage. You'll each make $50k in this scenario: You make $50k from selling it at $150k when you bought it for $100k, and they make $50k by replacing a $200k mortgage note with a $150k mortgage note.

Some people might say, "That's ridiculous. There's no way the former owners are ever going to pay $150k when they know you paid only $100k." But the people we've worked with are ecstatic because they've saved $50k and they got their house back, plus they may even have a massive amount of equity as a result.

BUTTER GUY

We won a single-family house in a foreclosure auction with the intention of flipping it. After we win a foreclosure, at least one of us always goes to the property in person to talk with the tenant and try to negotiate their exit. This time, we both went.

We go and knock on the door of the house we now own with the intention of having a conversation with the previous owner, who's still living there. This time, a guy comes to the door, and he's holding a stick of butter in his hand like an ice cream cone.

Kev's like, "Hi there."

And Butter Guy is like, "Yeah?" with an attitude while holding the stick of butter like a popsicle. He was clearly trying to blow us off and slam the door.

Then Kev says, "Wait, are you eating a stick of butter?"

Butter Guy kind of defensively answers, "No."

"Yes, yes you are," Kev says.

Butter Guy interrupts him. "If you want to talk to me, you can notice me. You can—"

"Dude, you're eating a stick of frickin' butter," Kev laughs.

Butter Guy kept trying to wave us off, and every time Kev just reminded him that he was standing in the doorway with a stick of butter covered in teeth marks in his hand. Finally, Butter Guy gave in.

Once he did, we found out that other people were living in the house with him—family members—who hadn't been on the original bank loan and who, as it turned out, had the ability to get financing to buy the house back from us. We'd been planning to flip the house anyway, not buy and hold, so once we knew that eligible, interested buyers already lived in the house, we were open to negotiating with them.

The deal ended up becoming one of our biggest successes: We bought the property, and put almost no money and very little time into it. While we were working out the details and they were getting the money together, we temporarily rented it to them and then literally converted them into buyers.

The lesson for us, and for you, is: Always look for the win-win. Sure, one of the occupants had just been foreclosed on. But until we talked with him, we had no idea there were other people with means in the house who hadn't been on the previous mortgage and had the ability to buy the house back. In this case, there was another path to making a profit while allowing the previous owner to stay in his house.

A key concept in buying properties this way is don't be super rigid. If you get an opportunity to make money in a different way with less investment of money and time, pivot your game plan. In this case, we were going to sell the house as a flip anyway. We would much rather sell it to the occupants. It's just that much easier. We don't care who we sell it to. Their money is just as green as somebody else's—and it's actually easier for us.

In this case, we were able to have a conversation and work a deal that all of us were thrilled with. We bought the house for

$60,000. We sold it to the occupants for $160,000—which was $100k less than what they had owed. We made $100k on the deal without really lifting a finger aside from knocking on the door, and they saved $100k without having to move. That's a win-win.

So, with these four options in mind, what started as a really weird, awkward, potentially combative and adversarial conversation with a former owner becomes a conversation about finding a solution for everybody in almost any scenario. The most important thing you can do in any of these situations is to have a conversation. Typically, if you buy a foreclosed house with people living in it, you need to figure out a way to get them out, which takes time and often money. A lot of foreclosure buyers would never knock on the door of the house they've just won, and they'd never have a conversation. They would just send an eviction notice and start kicking the occupants out. Guess what happens then? The occupants dig in. Now you've got a fight on your hands that could drag out for six months or a year. It doesn't have to be that way. If you keep these four solutions in mind—and you can probably come up with more if you're creative—you can often find the win-win.

When we've done this, the former owners/homebuyers hug us because they lowered their mortgage and they didn't have to move. And they basically got a free ride for quite some time while they weren't paying their mortgage. It's real. It's actual.

This solution might take three, four, even five months. But it feels good to help people keep their houses and lower their costs. It is the definition of a win-win for everybody.

CHOOSE YOUR OWN ADVENTURE

*If you're as stupid-crazy as we are and **this solution worked for you**, congratulations! Turn to page 301.*

*If **none of these crazy ideas worked** or you're not quite as crazy as we are, our condolences. Now turn the page.*

PURSUE AN EVICTION

At this moment in the process, we can pretty safely say: It sucks to be you.

If you have to pursue an eviction, go into this part of the process thinking "It's going to take six months to get the occupant out." If you can get it done faster, then bonus points for you. But otherwise, count on the eviction taking six months or even longer. That's because there are a lot of different ways people can slow the process down, like missing their hearing and then filing a motion to undo the default that they got by missing it, and then having a new hearing scheduled, and then going to that hearing and then filing for a continuance. It's a thousand little paper cuts, but it's a week here, a month there, and an extra two weeks there. It literally adds up.

DELAY, DELAY, DELAY

We bought an occupied property in Pittsfield, Mass, at a foreclosure auction. We closed in February. Five months later, we had yet to have a court hearing with the occupant, even though we started the eviction process shortly after we closed. Kev went out to the property a number of times. The former owner either wasn't home or pretended she wasn't home every time.

With no way to talk to her, we filed for eviction and got a hearing date, which got rescheduled and rescheduled and delayed and rescheduled again. Meanwhile, the former owner ignored us the entire time. Finally, before our hearing date in July, five months later, she emailed our attorney.

"Oh, no, I'm sorry. Today is Wednesday. Here's the email I've been sending to the court. I thought the case was in district court. They said it's housing court, but I've been trying to tell them I have a funeral to attend on my court date. So I can't go. Can we reschedule?"

Normally you might think, "Okay. I'm sorry about your grandmother. Sure. Fine. We'll see you in court next week then." But that's not the way the court does it. The court has to be available, the occupant has to be available, and our attorney has to be available. And a lot of times the courts are booked for weeks. So next week becomes three weeks. And maybe that's not going to work on our end, because our attorney is also booked up for other clients. So we won't have court now for a month. Her stall tactic of basically just saying, "Hey, I can't really show up because I've got a funeral to attend" will get her a one whole month of complete inaction. Meanwhile, we're eating holding costs, and she's paying us nothing for the use of the property.

The stones that occupants throw when they play this game build up an actual wall. They ignore, ignore, ignore. "Oh, I'll meet with you Friday," they say. But Friday becomes the next Tuesday, and then when Tuesday rolls around, they'll say, "Well, I didn't agree to meet with you." Or "I need more time to think about it." And "Let's talk again on Monday," and they just slowly stretch the whole process out. Before you know it, six months get away from you.

And then let's say we do go to court. We drive the hour there, and we pay our attorney to drive the hour there. Then the occupant doesn't show. She will lose by default. And then what happens next is actually worse.

Within a couple of weeks, she'll have her attorney file a motion to remove that default judgment with some kind of good reason behind it. The court here always wants to remove a default judgment if they have the ability to, so she gives them a decently good reason. Not like, "Oh, gosh. I had the sniffles." No, it's going to be like, "I had a funeral. I told the plaintiffs the day before that I had a funeral to attend and they said, 'no.' Here's the evidence that I had a funeral."

At that point, the judge will say, "Okay, yes, we'll remove it. Let's get you a new trial date." Then they'll schedule a new court date for three or four weeks out. We might as well just agree to reschedule now.

The time that it takes to finish an eviction can really add up, and in the meantime you're basically powerless. The best thing you can do is try to minimize the amount of time that the case drags on.

So, stonewalling. It's effective.

Whether they're bona fide tenants or not, Kev still tries to minimize the time it takes to get someone out of a property by setting clear expectations of the process, including the fact that the outcome is inevitable.

"It's just a matter of time," Kev will say. "It's going to happen. You are going to leave. It's just a matter of how long you're going to drag the process out and how much damage you're going to take doing it. So, if you fight me on this, here's what I will do."

Then he puts the cards right on the table. "We're going to file for eviction. We're going to take you to court. The judge will evict you.

It's just a matter of time, but the repercussions will be very damaging to you. We will burn a few months—three months, six months—and you'll have cheated me for six months of free living. In exchange, you're going to have an eviction on your record. You just got foreclosed on, so no bank is likely to give you a mortgage to buy another house right now. If you can't buy another house, you're probably going to have to rent one. Who's going to rent to you fresh off an eviction? Is it really worth getting three or six months of free rent for that? Why don't we just work this out? I'll still give you some time. Your record stays clean. I'll help you with some walking-away money, because I'd rather give you money than drag this process out for months and give the money to my lawyer. So, what do you say we work out a deal?"

The challenge is getting the person to listen. As soon as you say the word "eviction" or "judge," they're thinking, "How do I get an attorney? I can't get kicked out! My cousin told me they don't kick people out in December." They're not listening to the rest of the explanation. Not listening is the worst thing they can do in terms of moving a negotiation forward, so the goal is to get them to listen.

You need to think like a golfer and remember that you have many clubs in your bag. You don't *always* use the sand wedge when you play, but you want to have that club in your bag in case you're ever in a scenario where you really need it. If somebody's standing at a door yelling, you might say, "Listen, who the hell are you?" instead of being like, "Oh, I can see I caught you on a bad day, sir. I'm really sorry. Is there a better time we could talk about this?" It might be more effective in that moment to respond, "Excuse me? You're standing on *my* property telling me to get off *your* lawn? No, no, no. Let me set the record straight." That strategy has worked for us more often than you'd think.

We don't always escalate a situation, but we don't back away from it either when the situation calls for it. It takes a certain amount of skill to escalate people with the goal of then de-escalating. Sometimes folks respect and appreciate somebody matching their energy, standing up, and getting loud. We don't shout, but we do sometimes get aggressive back at a person who's getting aggressive with us. And they see, "Wow, that dog actually bites." Sometimes that realization will bring down the temperature in the situation.

A "TYPICAL" EVICTION

Let's just acknowledge at the outset that there is no "typical" eviction. But we want to give you a high-level description of what you might expect, with the very strong caveat that it will be different in your state. Even if you live in the same states where we operate, you'll have a different experience if you pursue an eviction, not only because the laws may be different by then, but also because the process evolves all the time. And no two eviction cases are ever alike. But on the theory that some information is better than no information, here goes.

In Massachusetts, it used to be that you would send a notice to the occupant at the beginning of an eviction. Then you'd file a notice of summary process with the court, and the court would set a date for a hearing in front of a judge a few weeks later. If you both wanted to, you and the occupant could sit down right before the hearing and talk about the case with mediators on staff at the housing court.

Kev loved it. Most people hate housing court in Mass, but Kev loved housing court because his goal with our bona fide tenants is never to kick somebody out. It's to stop them from stealing our services. When he's in court with a bona fide tenant, he's generally just looking to get the tenancy back on track and is usually willing to bend over backwards to do it. He likes to think he's a pretty fair guy, despite the comments he makes on TikTok. So before he's gone to an eviction hearing, he's usually already tried to work out a solution with them. He's called them. He's emailed them. He's stopped by and tried to have a conversation, "Hey, listen. You gotta get your rent caught up. What can we do? Can you pay a little bit more each month? How do we do this?" He wants to resolve it. And since the housing courts in Mass are staffed with professional mediators, it used to be that the landlord and the tenant could choose to sit down with a mediator before an eviction hearing with the hope of reaching a deal to get the tenancy back on track.

That process was helpful because tenants generally won't take action until they absolutely have to. They won't work with us as their landlords until the prospect of eviction becomes really real. And nothing's more real than walking into a courthouse for your eviction case in front of a black-robed judge. When that reality sets in, tenants—bona fide or not—are willing to take the situation seriously. Attitudes change on hearing day.

Now, however, mediation is forced into the process. Now when you go to court for the first time in an eviction case, you are not going to see a judge. Before the change, you were going to a hearing with a judge but if you wanted to take a few minutes before your hearing, you could sit with the mediator to try to work out your differences. With the new process, you don't get a hearing day when you first file your case. Instead, you get mediation day. Instead of going to the courthouse for a hearing in front of a judge, you're going to meet with a mediator. If you and the tenant can't work out a resolution with the mediator, only then will the court eventually schedule a hearing—which is going to be another month out. This new process takes out from the equation the motivation, the sense of urgency, the sense of dread that "Oh boy, maybe we should figure this out because it's going to go badly for me." It kicks the can down the road another month.

We don't know anything about the laws in your state, but the court system here is very geared toward tenants or occupants. Whether they're living in foreclosed property or not, it hands them an attorney. They're like the ambulance-chasing personal injury attorneys, but a housing law version of that. Some of them are okay-ish, in that they're not as blatantly ridiculous and deceptive as others, but Kev has experience watching them work with tenants. Some of the arguments they make are outlandish.

When we finally do get into the courtroom, the judge will often say, "Wait a minute, Mr. Tenant. You didn't fill out an answer form to countersue your landlord. And you missed your answer date for responding to the summary notice of eviction by a week. We can't have a hearing until you have filed an answer. Please go to the jury room and fill out an answer form."

We've argued, "Hold on, Judge. They can just fill it out right here in front of you. Even though they were supposed to fill it out last week and they should lose their right to counterclaim, here's the form. I've got a blank one they can fill out right here."

The judge will say, "No, they need to go to the jury room and fill it out. You're free to watch. Go to the jury room and you watch these people. Hold the tenant's hand, help them fill out this form."

Once we leave the courtroom and go into the jury room, the tenant will look over the form—usually for the first time. Then the tenant will ask, "So, what does this mean when it says, 'Do I have any claims against the landlord?'"

Then the free attorney who's been assigned to the tenant will pipe in, "Well, have you ever had a problem with your apartment in the time that you've lived there? Like, with the heat? Have you ever felt chilly in your apartment?"

What apartment has never had a maintenance issue?! But any maintenance issue or disagreement between us and the tenant will be whipped into a counterclaim, and now we're defending ourselves. That's why, in addition to being good people and good businesspeople, we have to be impeccable when we're dealing with tenants. Once we get in front of the judge, we need to be able to say, "We've done everything we're required to do as landlords and then some, Your Honor." When you're dealing with a tenant, imagine that somebody's watching you from their couch, watching the documentary of your experience. Imagine the judge is walking right next to you. You want the couch potato and the judge to have zero doubt that you did everything to avoid having to sue the person for eviction.

When it comes to foreclosures specifically, the attorneys will ask, "Did you get notice? Are you sure that you got noticed?" The attorneys basically position the case so the former owner can contest the foreclosure. First, they'll try to contest the foreclosure. Then they'll bring the bank in as party to the case, and it will take months to get a bank properly noticed about the case and into the courtroom.

Everybody's cam is on these days, so be aware that everybody can scrutinize every detail of your interactions. You have to have a compelling, justifiable reason for all your actions, and your actions must be reasonable in the eyes of the court and the court of public opinion. The standard is crazy high for the professional people—the banks, the lawyers, the foreclosure buyers, the landlords. In many states, like Mass, the standard is a lot lower for the homeowner. They have such a little standard, just a little bit of weight on their end of the scale. And they're like, "See? It balances out."

There are times, though, when you have no other choice. It's frustrating. It's infuriating. And yet when you're dealing with foreclosed properties, sometimes you come across people who just can't get out of their own way or yours. When that happens, pursuing an eviction is the last resort.

When you go down the eviction path, you really have to be prepared for…whatever comes, which is usually an ungodly amount of time, effort, and money before you get to the end. In the meantime, you're risking countersuits and incurring holding costs that can torpedo your investment. As landlords, we've sued more than a few people for eviction. We're now pretty familiar with the process, and pretty confident in our ability to win. And even still, we avoid it by exploring every possibility to negotiate a mutually agreeable solution. If all else fails, only then do we call Kev's handler, who also happens to be an exceptional housing lawyer. We don't go it alone, and neither should you.

CHOOSE YOUR OWN ADVENTURE

*If it's not too late to try **a crazy idea** to avoid suing for eviction, turn to page 270.*

*If it's not too late to try **a crazy idea** to avoid suing for eviction, turn to page 270.*

*If your only option is to **take your chance in housing court**, turn to page 307.*

*If your only option is to **take your chance in housing court**, turn to page 307.*

SECTION III
YOUR MOVE

CHAPTER 10

THE DEAL OF A LIFETIME

Kev grew up watching a lot of football. Jerry Rice was one of his favorite players, a receiver for the San Francisco 49ers in the '80s and '90s. He was not the biggest guy out on the field, but the dude would go to practice by himself before team practice started. Because he wasn't as physically big and gifted as everybody else, he was just a workhorse. And he became the best of the best in terms of his position by a wide margin because of his work ethic. He never gave up.

Kev grew up poor, but his advantage was seeing a dad who worked seventy hours a week so that Kev could have a little go-kart with a lawnmower engine on it. Kev didn't live with his dad, but his dad would come to Kev's house to cut wood and mow the lawn. He would do the dad things as best he could. Kev grew up seeing how his dad made it work and how a bad situation can be offset by working harder. Like getting up earlier and staying later at the gym, which Kev doesn't do—but Matt does. Those are the kinds of things that Jerry Rice would do and that Kev's dad would do.

That's how we've managed to build a thriving business. No matter what problem we've had—and we've had zillions of them—most of it was offset by saying, "Well, I guess we gotta work Sundays" or "You know, we'll just have to stay until midnight." We just worked away through most of our problems no matter how many times we screwed things up.

A key concept that we hope we've gotten across here is: Don't be super rigid in your game plan. *Don't be super rigid in your game plan.* Pivot your game plan when you have to. Much like water, find a path of least resistance. Remember that there are potentially several, if not many, ways to make money on a property you've just bought, so be willing to change up the game plan when the situation calls for it.

Maybe you're getting into foreclosure buying with the intention to buy and hold. You're like, "I know I want to start building passive income through rental property. So that's my goal: to go out, buy one house every year or maybe three units a year, and keep adding on. And after five years I'll have fifteen units or more, and that's my five-year plan." So now you go to foreclosure auctions with the goal of buying rental property. That's a great plan.

But if an opportunity presents itself where you could make $100k transactionally without creating passive income or investing the time and money to fix it and rent it and manage it, then you don't have to fight and kick this guy out and deal with the court process. You can just pivot the plan. Change your mind: "I know I was looking at buying rental property, but why don't I just treat this one like a flip? Because otherwise, to do the rental thing, I'm going to get resistance here, here, and here—and there's a different way presenting itself. So why don't I just do this one differently and I'll still not lose money. I'll make money."

We warned you at the beginning of this book that buying properties from foreclosure auctions is not for the faint of heart. Maybe you've gotten to this chapter, and it all seems like doom and gloom. You've gotten really overwhelmed, and now the process seems way more complicated and riskier than you ever imagined. But remember: If two bozos like us, just a couple of regular dudes, can figure this stuff out, so can you. You'll have us here every step of the way to help you reach your goal and be successful.

We started our business in 2008 because it really sucked making other people successful from our hard work. We knew that no matter how many hours we put in or performance goals we achieved, someone else would reap most of the benefits of our labor. We worked for people who sucked. And we'd do amazing. We'd crush it, and those people found success because we worked for them.

Working for ourselves has been awesome because now we receive the fruits of our labor, our effort, our risk. We found success because we're working for ourselves. We didn't necessarily get rid of a boss; now we have lots of bosses. We have a lot more responsibility and a lot more obligation and commitment. We have a lot more riding on our business than just punching a clock. Running your own business can be stressful and scary, but it's rewarding. You trade in one boss for ten bosses, who are your business partners and your employees. Okay, they're not really your bosses, but you're really, really, really obligated to their wellbeing. If you don't work hard, if you don't make payroll, things go really, really wrong for them. So in that respect, they're kind of in charge of your time and your life. But we're in charge of our destiny.

It's a powerful thing to be in charge of your destiny. We created this business, and now we create jobs. That's exactly what this country needs: people who are willing to not just support themselves, but also to put themselves in a role where they can help others find a path to support themselves.

And personally, it does offer us freedom we never would have had punching a clock. Even with all the commitments we have, more and more of our time is coming back to us—which we think is what it's really all about. Matt spends Wednesdays at home with his baby son, for example. Money is great and all, but if you don't have freedom, then money is meaningless.

Matt's also hoping that our business will create generational wealth for his family. As we write this, Matt's son Caleb is nine months old. Matt's goal is to buy him a two-family house someday, whether a foreclosure or another kind of distressed property. Matt plans to teach him how to run it so that eventually Caleb will inherit Matt's share of "the empire" we have built. Caleb can run it and hopefully grow it or do whatever he wants to do: maybe have other people manage it and just enjoy the income while he goes off and travels the world. We don't care. But building generational wealth for his son is a big part of why Matt does what he does.

We've met people at foreclosure auctions who were planning to buy property in the town where their kid was going to college. They wanted to buy a house in decent shape at a foreclosure auction, do a simple renovation, and then let the kid use it while going to school. After that, they planned to rent it out or resell it.

If that's you, we encourage you to go for it. Even if you've never bought a property before, armed with the right information, your first real estate transaction could be at a foreclosure auction. Now you can do it with eyes wide open and get a stellar deal. Roll your sleeves up. Do your due diligence. Watch us on YouTube and TikTok. And then make it happen.

WALK AWAY

One of Kev's favorite songwriters offered four classic pieces of life advice in the metaphor of a card game, and three of the four pieces were about leaving: "You gotta know when to hold 'em, know when to fold 'em, know when to walk away, and know when to run." How awesome is that?

Sometimes the hardest thing to do is to walk away when the going gets tough. We're all taught to keep going and never give up. "Winners never quit and quitters never win," right? That life advice might have worked for your middle-school gym teacher, but while we've got nothing against gym teachers, we'd rather take advice from Sun Tzu: "He will win who knows when to fight and when not to fight." If we had walked away from some of our deposits or had not raised our bid above our MAO to win an auction, we'd have been better off in several deals. The Fortress and the goat farm to name a few...

Hindsight is 20/20. It's hard to see that fact in the moment. But you have to be able to step back and look at what comes next. You have to take a moment to think, "So, if I do this, what happens next?" And that's really, really hard. If you're able to do that, you may decide to let that property go to another bidder or to walk away from a $10k deposit and save yourself $50k.

And believe us when we tell you: The best deal of all may be the deal you don't take.

CHOOSE YOUR OWN ADVENTURE

If you'd like to **pick yourself up, dust yourself off, and try again**, *turn back to the page where you left off and make another choice. Life may not give you do-overs, but we do!*

TAKE YOUR CHANCE IN HOUSING COURT

Despite all the wisdom that the Two Guys could impart from their years of buying foreclosed properties, you find yourself having to evict an occupant and hoping for the best.

How bad could it really be? you ask yourself skeptically. *Those Two Guys sound like jokers–albeit successful jokers. I'm sure if I just treat the entire court process with the dignity and respect it deserves, everything will turn out fine.*

It takes a week to hire an attorney, who requires a $1k retainer as a deposit toward their fee. Then it takes another week for the attorney to file the case, which also costs another $50 in filing fees and $50 for service of process on your tenant.

That's not so bad so far, you think. And you're lucky: You get a court date two weeks from the date you filed your case. The clock is ticking, but at this rate you should be done with the occupant in about six weeks, right?

The day before your court case, you remember to make the first $4k payment on your hard money loan. *Ouch*, you think. *I wouldn't want to have to make these payments for long with no money coming in.*

As you drive to court on the day of your eviction hearing, your attorney calls to say that the occupant requested an extension. Sadly, he sprained his back yesterday afternoon and had to go to the ER. He can't sit up straight and he's on painkillers. The judge agreed to delay for another week. You turn your car around, and drive by the property on the long way home. You could swear you see the occupant running through the sprinkler in the backyard….

The rescheduled hearing day finally arrives. You watch your phone anxiously all the way to the courthouse, and are relieved to see your attorney standing in the hallway outside the courtroom. She's talking to another lawyerly looking person in a suit. When she sees you, she gives you a "you won't believe this" sort of look. Your heart sinks almost as quickly as your bank balance.

"I just talked with the occupant's attorney," she says in an exasperated tone. "He hasn't heard from your occupant. We don't think they're showing up today."

Sure enough, the appointed time for the hearing comes and goes. Your attorney makes an excellent argument when she makes a motion for default judgment. The judge begrudgingly agrees.

You drive by the property again when you leave the courthouse, feeling victorious and imagining what the house will look like when the old peeling lilac paint is replaced with Benjamin Moore Wickham Gray. You pretend you're in Cash Cab and sing *I Like It* at the top of your lungs all the way home.

Then your attorney calls. She's heard from the occupant's attorney, and they requested a new hearing to vacate the default judgment. The judge agreed, so you're headed back to court again in another two weeks. Which means you can't evict the occupant for at least another two weeks—maybe three.

So much for having the property free and clear inside six weeks, you think to yourself.

You walk into the courthouse the following week and see your attorney standing outside the courtroom. She sees you and her eyes are THIS BIG. "What??" you ask.

"I think we may be dealing with a sovereign citizen," she says.

"A what?" you ask.

"I don't have time to explain," she says. "It's time to go inside the courtroom. They're calling our case."

You sit beside your attorney nervously as the judge addresses the litigants.

"Is everyone present today?" the judge asks.

"Yes, Your Honor," your attorney says.

You look over to the defense table where the occupant and his attorney are sharing an awkward silence.

"Your Honor," the attorney says. "My client has asked to represent himself. I request dismissal from this case."

"Is that right?" the judge asks the occupant. "You'd like to represent yourself? And you are…the occupant I presume?"

"I am the agent of the occupant."

"An agent of the occupant?" the judge asks. "Well, where is the occupant?"

"The occupant and I are one in the same, but I am acting as the agent of the occupant. And also the settler of the occupant," says the occupant. "But before this proceeding begins and I request my relief in equity, I'd like proof of jurisdiction."

"What the…" you whisper to your attorney.

"Shhhhhh!" she whispers back. "Just wait."

"This is housing court," the judge says, mildly perplexed. "What proof do you need?"

"Proof of jurisdiction!" the occupant exclaims. "I do not recognize the authority of this court to adjudicate my right to live in my property free to pursue happiness."

"The proof is the service of process you received from an agent of this court, and the laws of this great state," the judge says. "And the fact that I was elected by the people of this district to adjudicate these cases."

"That is insufficient proof! I do not recognize the authority of this court to remove me from the home I've lived in for fifteen years."

"Are you paying rent on this home?" The judge asks.

"I am not. I do not recognize the authority of the banks of this country to—"

"Okay, okay," the judge says. "Are you aware that a default judgment was entered against you last week in this case, because you did not appear at the hearing set for last week?"

"My person did not appear," says the occupant.

"Neither your person, nor your agent, nor your settler appeared," the judge says. "None of you was here, isn't that correct?"

"Well, I do not recognize the jurisdiction of this court to enter default judgment," the occupant says. "And therefore, I request the judgment be vacated."

"Well," says the judge slowly. "If I don't have jurisdiction to enter default judgment, I don't see how I can have jurisdiction to vacate the judgment. Request denied. Is there anything else?"

Sensing his error in logic, the occupant looks confused but remains silent.

"We are adjourned," the judge says.

Your attorney looks at you with a big smile. "Wasn't that fun?" she asks. "Want to go get a beer?"

But it's only 10:30 am, you think to yourself. "Yes, very much," you say.

On the way to the bar, you think about your next $4k hard money loan payment coming up in a week. Then you see your contractor left you a voicemail message while you were in the courtroom. He's taken another job while you've been evicting this occupant, and he can't get to your property until at least two months from now. You're grateful when your attorney picks up the tab.

Then you get her bill a week later, for another $1k.

Man, you think to yourself, *evictions are not for the faint of heart.*

CHOOSE YOUR OWN ADVENTURE

Don't give up now! *You're almost done! Turn to page 301.*

A PIECE OF TRASH

At long last, the house is yours, all yours. It's vacant. You have a marketable title. You own the deed. You're reflecting on your foreclosure adventure and all the lessons you learned along the journey. You're thinking, "I really owe it to those Two Guys for changing my life. I gotta send them an email to thank them. Maybe I'll name my firstborn after the really funny one." You're walking around the property lost in your reverie, checking the place out, feeling like the master of all you survey.

Suddenly, you stub your toe on something in the grass. You look down. It's that weird pipe again. You stubbed your toe on it the day of the auction and forgot about it. "Huh," you think casually, "I gotta remove that. But aside from that, the yard's pretty clean."

The next day you come back in your work clothes ready to remove that pipe and begin living the dream of homeownership. You pull on the pipe. It doesn't budge. Seems like a bigger job than you thought. You decide you'll hire someone who knows what they're doing.

The contractor you hire takes a look at the pipe and then gives you the bad news: That pipe in the yard actually goes to an underground oil tank. He tells you those things are expensive to remove, and very prone to leaking. After further inspection, he tells you he figures the cost of removal and remediation, as required by the EPA, will be close to $100,000.

You start feeling sick as you imagine telling the love of your life that you just accidentally bought a super-fund site that will cost your life savings and then some because you didn't realize what an underground oil tank meant. You just thought you'd stubbed your toe on a pipe.

POOF!

At long last, the house is yours, all yours. It's vacant. You have a marketable title. You own the deed. You're reflecting on your foreclosure adventure and all the lessons you learned along the journey. You're thinking, "I really owe it to those Two Guys for changing my life. I gotta send them an email to thank them. Maybe I'll name my firstborn after the really funny one." You're walking around the property lost in your reverie, checking the place out, feeling like the master of all you survey.

Key in hand, you walk to the front door. When you go to put the key in the lock, you notice the door isn't locked. In fact, it's slightly ajar. "Huh," you think. "Odd."

You open the door to your "new" property. You walk in, and get that eerie sense that something is not right. You feel the hot flush of panic setting in.

You go to the kitchen sink to splash cool water on your face, but when you flip open the tap, nothing. No water. The panic rises.

You try to calm yourself down. "Oh, right. They must have turned the water off. I'll just go down to the basement and turn it back on again."

You find the stairs to the basement and head down. And then the full picture emerges: There are no pipes. They've all been stolen. Those beautiful copper pipes that you saw right after you'd won the auction, when you were full of irrational exuberance over your victory, are gone. All gone. Along with your profit. And maybe your marriage.

TIME TRAVEL

"See?" you say to yourself right after you win your first foreclosure auction on that cute house in a great neighborhood. "I didn't need to do all that due diligence. All that stuff the Two Guys wrote about was just designed to sell their book. What's so hard? You find a foreclosure from your golfing buddy who's a real estate agent selling timeshares. You drive by, make sure it's vacant, walk inside, show up to the auction and, voila! Win yourself a $350k house for $35k."

You take a break from patting yourself on the back to sign the purchase agreement and write a $20k deposit check with the money you borrowed from your grandmother. You just know she won't regret investing in your new real estate venture with her savings from fifty years of selling eggs.

You call your college roommate who's now a lawyer in private practice to tell her the good news. "Congratulations!" she exclaims. "Happy to handle the closing for you."

Three days later she calls back.

"Did you run a title search on this property and research all the liens before you bought it?" she asks. You can hear the hesitation in her voice.

"Leans?" you ask. "Remind me what that means?"

"Liens are the debts that lead to a foreclosure, and there can be a lot of them. Did you know the foreclosure auction was for a second mortgage, not a first mortgage? Or that the first mortgage lien is $300k? And also that there's a property tax lien of $15k along with a $30k federal tax lien? Oh, and also there's a problem with the title."

"Gee, no," you say. "So, what does that mean?"

"It means you should say goodbye to that $20k deposit," she says.

314

"Damn," you think. "If only I could go back in time and finish my due diligence the right way!"

CHOOSE YOUR OWN ADVENTURE

*If you'd like to go back in time and **finish your due diligence the right way**, turn to page 159.*

SECTION IV
APPENDIX

GLOSSARY

After Repair Value (ARV) – The estimated future market value of a home after the completion of renovations.

Bank Foreclosure – The process of the lender repossessing a property as a result of the borrower failing to make mortgage payments.

Bona fide Tenant – A person who rents property from an owner for reasonable consideration under an arm's length agreement.

Buy-and-Hold – A passive investment strategy where the investor buys an asset and holds it for long periods regardless of market value.

Buy, Rehab, Rent, Refinance, Repeat (BRRRR) – An investment strategy in which investors buy a home, fix it up, gain passive income by renting it to a tenant, then use the equity to refinance. The process then repeats itself.

Cash for Keys – An agreement where the landlord offers money in exchange for a tenant vacating the rental unit.

Chain of Title – The historical record of ownership transfers for a specific piece of property.

Condominium Owners' Association (COA) – A legal organization of property owners in a condominium project that is responsible for maintaining the common areas and other elements of a condo development and for managing the association's finances and hiring vendors to clean, repair, and maintain the community with fees assessed from the property owners.

Conforming Loan – A loan to buy a property in which the terms conform to the standards of one of the government-sponsored enterprises Fannie Mae and Freddie Mac and which can therefore be resold in the secondary mortgage market, as compared with a "Nonconforming Loan."

Conventional Mortgage – A loan to buy a property in which the buyer makes a 20% down payment from their own resources in order to secure financing for the remaining 80% of the purchase price.

D-Box – Short for "distribution box," a key part of an electrical system.

Deed – A legal document that transfers the title of a property from one person to another.

Distressed Property – A home in need of significant repair and/ or is owned by a bank or other lienholder which is in the process of foreclosure.

Due Diligence – In real estate, an investigation before completion of a transaction to confirm facts or details about a potential investment, which may include: researching title, zoning, and other legal characteristics of a property; assessing the property's condition; and investigating liens.

Eviction – The process of expelling a tenant from a rental property.

Fix-and-Flip – An investment strategy whereby a purchaser remodels a property to add value and then immediately sells it for a profit.

Foreclosure – The process whereby a debtholder legally seizes the property that secures a debt after the debtor is unable or unwilling to make required payments on the debt.

Foreclosure Auction – The sale of a home that a lienholder has repossessed after which ownership is transferred to the highest bidder.

Hard Money Lender – A private individual or company willing to make a hard money loan and sees value in a potentially risky venture that would not generally be approved by a bank.

Hard Money Loan – A short-term, nonconforming loan generally used to fund the purchase of commercial or investment properties that doesn't come from a traditional lender and which typically carries a higher rate of interest than a conventional loan.

Home Equity Investment – A method of accessing a property owner's equity by selling a portion of the property's future value to an investor in exchange for a lump sum payment of cash.

Home Equity Line of Credit – A line of credit secured by a homeowner's equity in currently owned property.

Homeowners' Association (HOA) – A legal organization of property owners in a neighborhood that is responsible for maintaining the common areas and other elements of the neighborhood and for managing the association's finances and hiring vendors to clean, repair, and maintain the community with fees assessed from the property owners.

House Hack – An investment strategy that involves renting out portions of a residence to generate income.

Insurable Interest – An interest in a property sufficient to secure insurance that protects the holder from financial loss.

J-Box – An electrical junction box that protects electrical connections from the elements and protects people from electric shock.

Judicial Foreclosure – A foreclosure process wherein a lienholder brings suit in court for nonpayment against a debtor in an attempt to recover payment of the debt, and the resulting foreclosure auction is administered by a representative of the court.

Leach Field – (also known as a septic tank drain field) A series of underground perforated pipes, which removes contaminants from the septic tank.

Lien – The right to keep possession of a property that belongs to another person until that person's debt has been repaid.

Lienholder – (also known as a lienor) The individual or entity who holds the lien including but not limited to a mortgage lender, tax authority, homeowners' or condo owners' association, or contractor.

Lienor – *see* Lienholder.

Loan-to-Value (LTV) – An assessment of risk that lenders examine before approving a mortgage and generally expressed as a percentage of the value of the underlying property.

Long-term Rental – A rental property leased to a tenant for a period of longer than one month.

Marketable Title – A title that a reasonable purchaser would accept, assuming the property is free from claims and/or significant defects.

Maximum Allowable Offer (MAO) or Maximum Allowable Bid – The highest amount a purchaser can pay for a property and realistically expect to make a profit on their total investment including purchase cost, rehab cost, holding costs, and other costs.

Mechanic's Lien – A lien attached to a property as the result of a judgment against a homeowner for nonpayment of a contractor.

Mortgage – The most common method of financing real estate, a loan secured by the property that a borrower finances with the loan proceeds which may result in a lien on the property.

Multiple Listing Service (MLS) – An online database maintained by a group of collaborating real estate brokers that provides details about properties for sale.

Nonconforming Loan – As compared with a "Conforming Loan," a loan that doesn't meet the purchase standards of one of the government-sponsored enterprises Fannie Mae and Freddie Mac, which therefore can't be sold on the secondary mortgage market.

Nonjudicial Foreclosure – A foreclosure that does not involve a court, but instead allows a lienholder to sell the debtor's property to recover a debt that is owed.

Portfolio Lender – A lender who offers mortgages to investors but who does not sell those mortgages to other agencies.

Preforeclosure – The time period between the moment when the borrower defaults on the mortgage and when the lender forecloses on the property.

Private Lender – An individual or company who grants a loan to a buyer, as an alternative to a bank or financial institution.

Real Estate Owned (REO) – A property that is owned by the lender after failure to sell at a foreclosure auction.

Redemption Period – The period of time after a property has been sold at a foreclosure auction where the original homeowner can reclaim the rights to their home by paying the outstanding mortgage.

Reverse Mortgage – A borrowing agreement in which a homeowner exchanges equity in their home for regular periodic payments, typically to supplement retirement income.

Self-Directed IRA (SDIRA) – A type of Individual Retirement Account, whether traditional or Roth, that allows the owner to invest in a wider range of assets than the typical stocks, bonds, and mutual funds and which requires a custodian or trustee to hold the account's assets.

Short Sale – An asking price that is less than the amount due on the current mortgage.

Short-term Rental – A furnished space that is available for time periods of a few days to less than a month.

Spread – The gap between the cost of and profit on an investment.

Squatter – A person who unlawfully occupies a property without giving consideration to or receiving consent from the property owner.

Stack – Also known as a "plumbing stack," a pipe that directs all the wastewater out of a home and into a municipal sewer system or septic field.

Tax Deed – A legal document granting ownership of a property to a government body when the owner fails to pay property taxes, which is then generally sold to investors through an auction process. An investor who purchases a tax deed purchases the property.

Tax Lien Certificate – a certificate of claim against a property resulting from a lien for unpaid property taxes, which is then generally sold to investors through an auction process. An investor who purchases a tax lien certificate purchases the right to foreclosure and thereby secure ownership of the property.

Tax Lien Foreclosure – A foreclosure resulting from a property owner's failure to pay a property tax debt.

Title – In real estate, the aggregate of legal rights enjoyed by a property owner with regard to their ownership and possession of real property and signifying absolute ownership.

Use and Occupancy – A formal agreement between the property owner and an occupant that allows the occupant to occupy or use the property for a specific period of time without creating a tenancy.

Wholesale – An investment strategy where the wholesaler gains a property under contract, then finds a buyer who is willing to pay a higher price, allowing the wholesaler to keep the profit.

ACKNOWLEDGMENTS

I would like to acknowledge my wife, all our staff, and our contractors for putting up with us for so long and helping us through the tough times. – Matt, "The Flippin' Ninja"

My thanks to friends and family for their patience and support, even though they didn't fully understand what we were doing. At one point my dad loaned us his old pickup truck and gave us a car with a salvaged title for our work vehicles. He even tossed us $20 here and there for gas. Thanks also to the team of staff and professionals we've found over the years who really are the main reason anyone thinks we're competent. And finally, thanks to the social media followers who've reached out to share the motivation they've gotten from our videos and to update us on their successes and challenges. – Kevin, "The Property Prince"

ABOUT THE AUTHORS

Matthew Tortoriello and Kevin Shippee are successful entrepreneurs, real estate investors, students, and mentors based in Springfield, Massachusetts. Through trial and oh so many errors, they have learned firsthand about all the pitfalls and opportunities of buying distressed properties, particularly via foreclosure auctions.

Matt (a.k.a. The Flippin' Landlord Ninja) has used his determination and ninja warrior skills to help acquire and rehab hundreds of properties over the last fifteen years, all while building a great workplace for more than twenty-five employees. When he's not scoping out real estate, he enjoys training for American Ninja Warrior and spending time with his wife, Kristen, and son, Caleb.

Kevin (a.k.a. The Property Prince) has used his communication skills and love of animals (despite wicked allergies) to navigate hundreds of landlord-tenant relationships, both in and out of various court systems. When not working, he enjoys spending time with his pet rabbit, Mischief, and reading scratch & sniff versions of 17th Century romantic poetry.

Matt and Kev are passionate about helping others learn from their successes and failures in real estate and business!

Ready to dive in further and learn more
from the Two Guys as they take on Real Estate?

instagram.com/twoguystakeonrealestate

tiktok.com/@twoguystakeonrealestate

facebook.com/twoguystakeonrealestate

youtube.com/@TwoGuysTakeonRealEstate

twitter.com/2guystake